CURRICULUM TECHNOLOGY

CJ Investigations in the USA

WRITTEN BY:
Larry Adkisson

EDITOR:
Jennifer-Lynn Jennings

D1401355

CHANNEL CUSTOM PUBLISHING

Photography: Curriculum Technology, LLC and iStockphoto®

Author Photo: Courtesy of Jessica Adkisson

Publisher: Channel Custom, 3520 Seagate Way, Suite 115, Oceanside, CA 92056.

Manufactured in the United States of America, 1st edition, Curriculum Technology, LLC, 2011.

CJ Investigations in the USA. A textbook by Curriculum Technology, LLC.

Oceanside, CA. 1st edition, 2011.

ISBN 978-0-9837570-1-6

WARNING: Re-creation of any case study or event listed in the materials may result in injury or
property damage if extensive care is not taken at all times. Curriculum Technology and Channel

Publishing are not responsible for any injuries or damage to property that may occur from the use
of referenced equipment or any other supplies.

Experiments and activities derived from this book should be conducted with oversight by, and at
the direction of, a qualified instructor.

***

Table of Contents

About the Author

Larry Adkisson

Larry Adkisson has over thirty-five years of law enforcement and investigative experience. He was the Lieutenant of Investigations for the Douglas County Sheriff's Department (Colorado), and was an investigator for the Arapahoe County (Colorado) and the Denver County District Attorney's Offices. Adkisson was a patrol officer with the Phoenix, Arizona and Lakewood, Colorado police departments. He also served as a corporate security investigator for SafeCo Insurance.

Adkisson has taught at police/sheriff's academies throughout Colorado and is currently an adjunct instructor at ITT-Tech. He has a master's degree in Criminal Justice from the University of Colorado.

Adkisson is currently the investigator for the DNA Project with the State of Colorado Attorney General's Office.

Dedication

I dedicate this book to all of the wonderful mentors I had throughout my law enforcement career who taught me the importance of using the following qualities "on the job:" compassion, integrity, and excellence. This is also for all of the students who are the future of law enforcement, corporate and private investigations. Finally, and most importantly, this is dedicated to my family. My wife is not only my best friend; she is my strength and joy. Her proofreading and editing helped create this book. Our three daughters are our joy and the source of my greatest pride.

MODULE 1

Introduction to Investigations

Key Module Concepts:

- The primary goals of an investigation

- What constitutes a criminal investigation

- The concepts and relevance of "inductive reasoning" and "lateral thinking"

- Three examples of the psychological and physiological effects that investigators face

- The importance of compiling reports in a timely manner

Introduction

A corporate security investigator is assigned to look into the theft of laptop computers from various offices within a company. The company wants the investigation to be both quick and discreet.

A patrol officer is dispatched to a domestic violence situation. At the scene, the officer finds the front door ajar; nothing can be heard from within the house. He steps inside and immediately observes signs of a struggle. Blood is on the walls and floor. In the master bedroom, the officer finds a woman standing in a corner. At the foot of the bed is the body of a deceased male who appears to have been stabbed numerous times.

A private investigator is hired to look into the death of a client's son. The private investigator learns that the son was found in his own bedroom with a single gunshot wound to the head. The decedent's girlfriend was in the bedroom at the time of the shooting. The police investigation concluded the death was a suicide. However, the client believes his son was killed by his girlfriend.

An insurance investigator investigates a motor vehicle accident claim in an attempt to determine who was at fault. The claim exposure is in the millions of dollars. Both drivers were killed in the accident.

What do these investigations have in common? How are they different? Do the goals of each investigation differ?

The most common image of an investigation is of a criminal investigator or detective working a homicide scene. Movies, television, and modern literature feed into that image. Homicide investigations are but one example of the types of investigations that are conducted hundreds of time every day. Some are law enforcement related, while others are not.

Traditional investigations textbooks tend to center on criminal investigations, usually emphasizing homicides. In reality, only a small percentage of investigators ever become homicide investigators or work on homicide cases. There are numerous investigation-related careers, both within and outside the field of law enforcement.

This text centers on investigative principles and concepts that apply to both criminal and civil investigations.

Ask Yourself

- *What does it take to conduct a thorough investigation?*
- *Are there special traits that investigators possess?*
- *Are there distinctions between criminal and civil investigations?*

Criminal and Non-Criminal Investigations

Think about your favorite detective show. It starts with the discovery of a crime and through the course of the show establishes who committed the crime. In the classic sense, an investigator is the detective who comes into the investigation after the patrol officers respond to a scene. They are the seasoned law enforcement officers who wear "plain clothes" and work in a detective bureau.

In reality, an **investigator** is anyone who works on any aspect of an investigation, including fact finding and collection of evidence. Therefore, patrol officers, crime scene technicians, and the coroners are all investigators.

The word "investigate" comes from the Latin term *vestigare*, which means to track or trace. Central to all investigations is the principle of working from the unknown to the known. Successful investigations are dependent upon the investigator's ability to reconstruct what occurred. This requires a great deal of patience, fortitude, and people skills. Seasoned investigators readily concede that the ingredients to solve cases include luck, combined with knowledge, experience, and hard work. Investigators also gather clues from the criminal's mistakes and the evidence he/she leaves. Although investigators learn from the cases they work, no two crimes are alike.

What's That Term?

The phrase "criminal investigations" is synonymous with law enforcement agency-related investigations that have the primary goal of identifying and holding accountable violators of the law. Criminal investigations may also involve non-law enforcement personnel, such as private investigators, public defender investigators, and corporate investigators.

A crime is an act or omission of an act in violation of penal law. Crimes are punishable by a fine, imprisonment, or death. The **criminal statutes** that are violated during the commission of a crime may be municipal, state, or federal. A **criminal investigation** is an inquiry that looks into violations of those statutes. Law enforcement officers are empowered to investigate cases that fall within their jurisdiction. For instance, police and sheriff's departments can investigate violations of municipal and state statutes, while federal agents investigate violations of federal statutes. If the situation does not constitute a violation of a criminal statute, then no crime was committed.

Sometimes the initial information discovered is insufficient to determine whether a crime was committed. A situation is investigated until it can be decided whether or not a crime occurred. If it is determined that a crime was not committed, law enforcement ceases its investigation.

In non-criminal investigations, the focus is on exonerating an innocent person or determining civil liability. Civil violations do not result in incarceration. Insurance companies, large corporations, and private investigators conduct investigations that may result in the filing of criminal charges, but private investigators do not have the authority to make arrests.

One important distinction between law enforcement investigations and non-law enforcement investigations deals with the standards of proof (also known as burdens of proof). A **standard of proof** refers to the requirement that must be met in order for a prosecutor to prove his or her case. In criminal proceedings, the standards of proof are reasonable suspicion, probable cause, and beyond a reasonable doubt. **Reasonable suspicion** is the standard that must be met to justify the officer's initial contact with a person; it is also the standard for some court orders. **Probable cause** is the standard that officers/investigators must meet before an arrest can be made. **Beyond a reasonable doubt** is the standard that must be met for an individual to be convicted of a crime. These are standards that non-law enforcement investigators do not have to worry about. Non-criminal investigations may center on questions of liability, security issues, and violations of policy and procedure. The standard of proof in a civil investigation is called preponderance of the evidence; this establishes that there is more than 50% chance that a party committed an act.

Criminal investigations have heavier standards of proof because the consequences are higher. A person convicted of a crime may face incarceration. Civil investigations carry a lesser burden of proof because the consequences are monetarily based and cannot result in incarceration.

While criminal and non-criminal investigations have their own unique aspects, they share a number of common traits. An investigator's actions and observations during the initial phase of the investigation set the stage and impact the remainder of the case. In criminal investigations, the investigator's actions will be critiqued, analyzed, and dissected by the defense counsel, the prosecution, and the command staff of the law enforcement agency. Non-criminal investigations have a different audience, but have similar goals of determining what occurred, who is accountable, and taking the appropriate action. Non-criminal investigators also have many of the same functions and responsibilities. They must preserve all evidence, determine who committed the act (a crime or other act), compile concise reports that will be presented in court or to another audience, and strive to be objective.

Primary Goals of an Investigation

The primary goals of a criminal investigator include:

- Preserve any and all evidence

- Establish that a crime has or has not been committed

- Establish proof of who committed the crime

- Compile information that can be used in a court of law

- Exonerate those who didn't commit the crime

- Be objective in the investigation of the case

Pro-Active and Reactive Investigations

Reactive investigations are usually initiated in response to either a dispatch call or an observed potential criminal violation. This type of investigation is most commonly associated with patrol officers.

Pro-active investigations are planned in advance and are initiated by law enforcement. Examples include undercover drug operations, "sting operations," Internet investigations, and vice cases.

The major difference between the two is that reactive investigations are more spontaneous and are initially beyond the control of the investigator. Reactive investigations involve varying degrees of time between when the crime or act occurred and when the investigator becomes involved. The resulting time gap may have a profound impact on the success or failure of the investigation. Reactive investigations require the ability to ascertain what is occurring, who is responsible, and how to respond. Sometimes the investigator is required to make split-second decisions on how to proceed.

Pro-active investigations are usually easier to control because the investigator has more control over the situation. There is often a great deal of planning and discussion prior to a pro-active investigation. Sometimes things don't go according to plan and the investigator has to make split-second decisions, but often there is a contingency plan in place.

Non-law enforcement investigators conduct both pro-active and reactive investigations; the vast majority of investigations are reactive. For instance, corporate security investigators may be asked to conduct a sting in order to ascertain who stole corporate assets or embezzled funds. A Public Defender's Office investigator is asked to interview potential witnesses. These are all examples of reactive investigations.

Contrary to what is portrayed on television, statistics show that the majority of investigations are a result of witnesses, victims, or even suspects making a call to the relevant law enforcement agency, and the agency dispatching an officer in response.

Television and movies provide a frame of reference for "crimes in progress." Someone contacts the police. Police dispatch sends patrol cars to the scene. Crimes in progress can also occur when an officer or detective sees a crime being committed. The majority of crimes in progress calls originate through calls to dispatch. Non-law enforcement investigators seldom deal with "crimes in progress."

Although non-law enforcement investigators are seldom the initial responders, a working knowledge of how crimes in progress are handled provides valuable insight concerning if the investigation was done properly.

Universal Themes

All investigations have certain universal themes. This applies to both law enforcement and non-law enforcement investigations. These universal themes will help any investigator conduct a thorough investigation and provide a professional work product.

FIGURE 1.1: *An effective investigator pays attention to all the details at the scene.*

Attention to Detail

Think of your favorite television or literary investigator. A major trait this investigator likely has is the ability to pay attention to details, especially things other people seem to miss. Literary character Sherlock Holmes epitomized this characteristic.

For the contemporary investigator, attention to detail is comprised of two components. The first is associated with "taking in the whole scene." A good investigator both sees and observes. An example of seeing, but not observing is looking in the refrigerator and not finding the ketchup, even when it is sitting at eye-level on the shelf. Was the suspect right or left-handed? Were the items on the night stand next to the bed consistent with the victim suffering from a cold? Finding that the screen door to the residence is locked from the inside, a great deal of mail is still in the victim's mailbox, newspapers from the last four days are on the driveway, and the victim's vehicle is in the garage are important observations to support that something may be wrong.

The second component of attention to detail relates to documentation of the investigation. Reports should contain all of the details associated with the investigation. It is not only important to "see" but to "articulate" what was seen. Articulation is the ability to effectively convey observations so that others can understand exactly what the investigator saw. This component will be discussed in more detail in the section dealing with documentation.

Effective investigators sweat the small stuff. They take photographs and measurements of each piece of evidence collected. They look for changes in speech patterns, facial characteristics, and inconsistencies in statements. They notice if a person is right or left-handed, which wrist he/she wears a watch on, and the nature of his/her interaction with other people.

Documentation

An old axiom in law enforcement is "If it is not in your report, it didn't happen." Investigators are often called upon to testify concerning what is in their reports. If the investigator testifies about information not discussed in the reports, attorneys for the opposing side may attack the investigator's documentation. It is not uncommon for attorneys in that situation to ask the rhetorical question, "Then what other information is not in your report?" The investigator will also be asked what criteria he/she used in selecting what would, or wouldn't, be contained in the investigator's report. This is one means by which opposing counsel attempts to establish investigator bias. As you can imagine, this results in a very uncomfortable situation for the investigator who is testifying, and can create doubt with the jury.

The failure to document accurately and thoroughly goes beyond testifying in court. Other investigators rely upon information provided in earlier reports for direction. If the information in the initial reports is incomplete or inaccurate, the investigator handling the subsequent portion of the investigation will spend time addressing information that has

FIGURE 1.2: *Reports can make or break a case, so be sure to thoroughly and accurately document all aspects of the investigation.*

already been obtained but was not documented, or may go down a misguided path of investigation. This may cause the investigation to reach incorrect conclusions, or make the investigator look inept.

Privately hired investigators are paid to provide documentation that is professional and complete. Corporate or private investigators who provide incomplete reports will find themselves without a job or clients. Conversely, the investigator who writes thorough and complete reports will get referrals or additional work, because the client knows the product is complete and thorough. For instance, a good practice for ensuring accurate information is to let the interviewee read your completed report after an interview. If the report contains all of the pertinent information of the interview, the rapport between the interviewer and interviewee is enhanced. It also affords an early opportunity to correct any mistakes or misconceptions that may be contained in the report.

An ongoing dilemma for any investigator is what should be in a report. If the report contains everything that occurred, the material will be too voluminous. If it contains nothing but "the bare bones" then the report will be viewed as incomplete. The investigator must document everything that helps explain or describe a given situation, while information that is unnecessary or superfluous is omitted. Unfortunately, there are no simple guidelines that apply to every given situation.

There are several common mistakes relating to documentation. One of the most common errors is the failure to properly quote important statements by witnesses, suspects, or victims. What if the witness said, "I am going to make sure you never cheat with another woman again," and the investigator wrote, "The suspect said he was going to kill the victim?" Doesn't the victim's actual quote give a different picture than the investigator's paraphrase? Not everything needs to be set off by quotation marks, but all significant statements should be documented fully. The trick is learning when to quote a statement and when to summarize it.

Another common error associated with documentation relates to measurements. Whenever possible, take accurate measurements and indicate the measurements in your report. If exact measurements are not taken, make sure the report reflects that any figures are an approximation.

Unbiased and Impartial

All investigators must strive to be both unbiased and impartial in their observations and documentation. This not only helps ensure that the investigator obtains an accurate picture of what occurred; it also helps the investigator keep an open mind. If an investigator is biased and/or partial to one position over another, a filtering of information occurs. That filtering may be intentional or unintentional. Filtering of information distorts the picture of what actually happened.

What's That Term?

*To be **unbiased** means to be fair, and free of any prejudice or favoritism. To be **impartial** means to treat all aspects of the case equally. Ideally, all investigators should be geared toward learning what actually occurred.*

Investigator bias occurs when an investigator maintains information that is favorable to his/her theory of the case, and withholds or disregards information that contradicts that theory. For instance, in criminal cases, the investigator may believe that a certain individual committed a crime, but the evidence doesn't support that contention. The emotional aspects may be so strong that the investigator disregards information that negates the premise that a given suspect committed the crime.

Sometimes in non-criminal cases, investigators are hired to verify information. If the investigator is hired to document that a high-ranking employee is selling trade secrets, the investigator may feel great pressure to put together a case supporting that premise. The professional investigator is able to compartmentalize that pressure and stay objective.

It is important to remember we all hold biases and stereotypical views. The trick is to keep these views in check while conducting an investigation. When an investigator is alleged to be biased or partial, the best defense against the allegations is to prove that this is not the case. Showing that the investigator followed all leads and documented all information, including information that was not favorable to the investigator's case, is an effective means of showing an unbiased investigation.

Being unbiased and impartial is a critical component for the investigator during the investigation, but it is just as critical when the information is presented to a jury or some other audience. Juries don't believe investigators who have done biased investigations.

Providing a Professional Product

What is a professional product? In law enforcement, a professional product consists of two components: the investigation and the reports associated with the investigation.

Patrol officers are expected to conduct initial investigations that provide complete, concise, and understandable information. Reports should reflect sound judgment as to whether a crime occurred and, if a crime did occur, the nature of the offense. If a patrol officer fails to meet this standard, the case may be compromised and the officer's chances of advancement will be greatly impacted. An officer's chances for advancement are often tied to both his writing ability and the ability to be a logical, organized thinker.

Detectives represent their law enforcement agencies with a wide range of audiences. How they deal with victims, coordinate investigations within their own department, and interact with the District Attorney's Office are important aspects of the functions associated with detectives.

An investigator's work is constantly evaluated by peers, law enforcement command staff and the courts. If the investigator doesn't provide a professional product, several major consequences may occur:

- The right suspect is not identified or arrested

- A person may be wrongly accused of a crime he didn't commit

- The public image of the department is tarnished

- The District Attorney's Office cannot proceed with the case

- The jury will not have all of the information they need to make an informed decision concerning the case

- The career of the investigator may be negatively impacted

These concepts apply to both law enforcement and non-law enforcement investigators. Non-law enforcement investigators are often paid a great deal of money to conduct investigations, and clients expect quality work for their money.

Timeliness and Continuity

Every investigation is different. Therefore, the amount of time needed to properly work an investigation varies on a case-by-case basis. Some investigations may be solved within hours, while other investigations take months. Some cases are never solved. The **timeliness** of a case is determined by what had been done over a given period of time. Were viable leads pursued in an efficient and opportune manner? Were reports compiled within a reasonable period of time?

Timeliness does not necessarily relate to the time it takes to complete a case, or even whether the case is solved. If an investigator puts off working a specific case because it was not interesting or the investigator did not like some aspect of the case, then the investigation cannot be completed in a timely fashion, even it if is eventually solved. However, if the investigator has developed all leads as far as the leads can go and the case is not solved, then the investigation can still be considered timely.

Reports should be completed as quickly as possible, with twenty-four hours as the maximum amount of time it takes to file a report. If an investigator is working a major case, reports should be done the same day as the information is obtained, especially if the case relates to the safety of the public (for instance, a homicide suspect or a sexual predator). Information obtained from one investigator may be important to other investigators working the same case.

Furthermore, if a report is written twenty-four hours or more after the investigator learned the information, opposing counsel may contend that the investigator's memory was not as accurate when the report was written as it was when the information was first obtained, or that the investigator has an ulterior motive for the delay in writing the report. This is especially true if the interview was not recorded or videotaped. Writing the report as soon as possible shows professionalism, avoids allegations of faulty memory and/or ulterior motives, and helps other parties associated with the investigation move forward.

Continuity refers to working a case until it is resolved. An investigator may be working multiple cases, but the investigator does some work on all of the cases, without neglecting one in favor of another. If an investigator does not work on a specific case consistently because it was not interesting or the investigator did not like some aspect of the case, then there is no continuity to the investigation.

Inference, Opinion, and Facts

In the attempt to reconstruct what occurred, all investigators deal with facts, inferences, and opinions.

A **fact** is something that is known with certainty. Some examples of facts: The sun rises in the east and sets in the west. Tuesday always follows Monday. The majority of people are right-handed.

Inferences are different from facts. Inferences are conclusions drawn from facts. For example, footprints in the snow infer that someone walked in that location since it snowed. Facts and inferences are not the same thing.

Opinions are based upon life experiences, education, and feelings. There are lay opinions and expert opinions. An example of a **lay opinion** is that anyone who kills people is a psychopath. A psychiatrist who specializes in psychopathic personalities would be able to provide an **expert opinion** concerning a particular homicide suspect's being psychopathic state.

Sometimes an inference, even when based upon facts, may be incorrect. When an interviewee has poor eye contact, moves around a lot in their chair, and appears nervous, the interviewer may conclude that the person is lying. In reality, the person may be shy, have a physical disability, or just an aversion to being in a police department. An incorrect inference could be detrimental to an investigation.

Investigators should avoid giving opinions in formal reports unless the investigator is rendering an opinion as an expert. Rather than giving an opinion, a trained investigator will gather facts and make inferences, with the caveat that the inference may not be correct and is subject to change if and when more facts are obtained. It is far too easy for an opinion to be treated as fact.

Lateral Thinking/Inductive Reasoning

Conducting an effective investigation requires more than collecting and analyzing evidence. Investigators constantly form conclusions based upon information they obtain during the course of an investigation. For instance, a patrol officer responds to the scene of an accident and sees two vehicles in an intersection. One vehicle has damage on the driver's side of the vehicle, while the other vehicle has damage on the front of the vehicle. In the grill of the second car is paint transfer that matches the color of the first vehicle. The officer concludes that the second car collided with the first car. This is an example of **inductive reasoning**. Based upon observations associated with the accident, the officer came to a broad generalization, or a theory. This is also referred to as the "bottom up" approach.

The use of inductive reasoning is what separates great investigators from the pack. Effective inductive reasoning requires the ability to "take in" all of the information at the crime scene, as well as the ability to modify conclusions when additional information becomes available. Both law enforcement and non-law enforcement investigators use inductive reasoning when working their cases.

In another example, a uniformed officer arrives on a scene and finds a woman who has multiple bruises to her arms and legs. With the victim is a male who is being belligerent and uncooperative. The officer's initial conclusion may be that the male caused the injuries to the victim. As the officer obtains more information, the **initial conclusion** (a theory based upon the facts immediately available) may become modified. This process results in the forming of a **hypothesis** as to what occurred. Unlike the initial conclusion, the hypothesis is constantly reviewed and may change as additional information becomes available. If the hypothesis is that the male assaulted the female and the obtained information supports that hypothesis, the officer arrests the male. If additional information causes the investigator to conclude the male did not commit the act, the investigation continues.

In the words of Sherlock Holmes, a hypothesis should fit the facts, rather than the facts fitting a hypothesis. If an investigator is working a case and forms a hypothesis that doesn't take all of the information into consideration, the hypothesis is faulty. Sometimes an investigator may become so invested in a case that he filters or ignores any information that doesn't fit his theory. In such situations, the investigator may not obtain a true picture of what occurred. The use of a hypothesis is an effective means of evaluating a case and determining whether the conclusions are sound or faulty.

Lateral thinking is the ability to think outside the box. Lateral thinkers must reason through a situation, using solutions that are not immediately obvious or attainable through the use of traditional logic. This is another invaluable tool to the investigator.

Example: A series of burglaries and sexual assaults occurred in a specific neighborhood.

Traditional logic would lead the investigator to interview witnesses, conduct a neighborhood canvass, and interview the victim(s).

The investigator who utilizes lateral thinking would do the aforementioned actions, but would also check for any parking tickets, field contacts, or documentation of suspicious activity in that neighborhood during the time period of the assaults. The lateral thinker is always asking questions and utilizing creative approaches.

Communication

Both written and verbal communication skills, as well as the ability to interpret body language, are critical traits in an investigator. An effective investigator must be able to interact with a wide range of personalities in order to obtain information. Once the information has been obtained, the investigator must be able to effectively communicate it to others. The inability to communicate can have a devastating effect on the investigation, because an investigator's professionalism is often tied to his or her ability to communicate, especially in their reports.

Communication is comprised of two major components: the person doing the communicating and the person who is receiving the communication. **Filters** are factors that interfere with effective communication. Some examples of filters are background noise, multi-tasking, thinking about something else, and not understanding what the person is saying.

Other filters that can greatly impact communication include cultural differences, socioeconomic status, educational level, defense mechanisms, and emotions. Effective communicators recognize potential filters and work to overcome them. Building rapport, speaking on the same level (without being condescending), recognizing cultural considerations, and maintaining a calm demeanor may lessen the effects of filters.

Effective communication also requires **feedback**, which occurs when the listener responds to the speaker. This reinforces that the listener actually received the message. By way of example, two men are talking about last night's football game. The "speaker" talks about how well the quarterback performed in the game. The "listener" responds that he thought the quarterback was one of the best in the league.

Reflective listening is a type of feedback in which the listener summarizes the information received. This is a very important tool for the investigator, as it is imperative that the investigator not only obtains information, but that the information is accurate. Reflective listening allows the initial speaker to rectify any "incorrect" information that the listener may have received.

Executing written forms of communication are an essential part of being an investigator. Law enforcement investigators are constantly writing offense and interview reports, search warrants, arrest warrants, and memoranda. Non-criminal investigators routinely write reports concerning their activities and observations. Investigative reports are reviewed by a variety of audiences that often take action based upon those reports. If you are unable to communicate effectively in your reports, you will not be a successful investigator. The ability to write proper reports is not only critical to the success of any investigation; it is often tied to career advancement. The communication must be concise, clear, and grammatically correct.

Most of our communication is non-verbal. Non-verbal communication, or body language, includes social distance, facial expressions, eye contact, hand movement, tone of voice, body positioning, and body posture. Clothing may also play a major role in our non-verbal communication; for instance, a person's attire and accessories can provide insight into their socioeconomic status or affiliation with a certain group.

The effective investigator is constantly looking for non-verbal clues as to sincerity, deception, or interest. But it is important to remember that while the investigator is reading non-verbal cues, the people being contacted are also reading the investigator's non-verbal clues.

Effective interviewers are cognitive of this and strive to have their non-verbal clues match their verbal information.

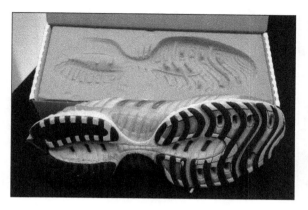

FIGURE 1.3: *Both law enforcement and non-law enforcement investigators must understand the relevance of different types of evidence.*

Direct and Circumstantial Evidence

During the course of any investigation, investigators obtain direct and circumstantial evidence. The majority of the evidence obtained is direct evidence, but direct evidence does not always equate to being the best evidence. **Direct evidence** is witness testimony about what the witness saw or heard. Contrary to popular belief, witness testimony is not the most reliable evidence. People's memories wane with time, and sometimes information changes from interview to interview. People also may not be totally candid during their interviews. They may have vested interests in the case, such as being friends with the victim or the suspect. Poor eyesight, poor hearing, and other physical conditions may also impact a person's observations.

Circumstantial evidence is a fact that can be used to infer another fact. Blood found at a scene can be used to infer whether the defendant was at the scene. Examples of circumstantial evidence are blood, weapons, imprints/impressions, hair/fibers, tool marks, and questioned documents. While circumstantial evidence may not seem as strong as direct evidence, some circumstantial evidence is better than direct evidence. For example, the defendant's DNA found on the victim or on her clothing can be very compelling evidence, especially if there is no logical explanation as to how the suspect's DNA got on the victim or her clothes.

FIGURE 1.4: *It is vital that all investigators know how to collect, identify and preserve evidence.*

Today's juries anticipate that scientific evidence will be presented during court proceedings. Jurors expect investigators to find fingerprints, blood, and other circumstantial evidence at a scene. This is commonly referred to as the "CSI Syndrome". When no circumstantial evidence is presented, juries often conclude that the investigation was faulty.

Evidence Protection

In criminal cases, **chain of evidence** refers to how evidence was handled from the time it is seized until it is presented in court. The prosecutor must show to the court that the evidence was not compromised or altered.

All investigators should be trained in the proper identification, collection, and preservation of evidence. All evidence should be properly packaged, sealed, and identified; failure to do so could result in the evidence not being introduced at trial. Failure to properly preserve evidence could also have a devastating impact on any testing. A DNA sample that was not properly preserved could return inconclusive lab findings. If the DNA sample was the only hard evidence tying the suspect to the crime, the case could be lost.

Maintaining the integrity of the evidence also applies to civil proceedings. The importance of protecting seized evidence cannot be overstated. This not only applies to drugs, blood, semen, saliva, and other bodily fluids, but also to videos, CDs, and audiotapes.

The Perfect Investigation

Some investigations are better than others, but none are perfect. An investigator should strive to conduct the perfect investigation, even though such a goal is unattainable. The success of an investigation is often tied to what investigators learn from people, the investigator's ability to recognize evidence, the ability to work all aspects of the case, and some degree of luck.

When there is a delay in reporting the crime, little or no physical evidence may be available. Testimony of lay witnesses then becomes the focal point of the investigation. Sometimes suspects leave few or no clues, and investigators must be patient and persistent in their investigation. Some investigations are concluded within a couple of hours, others may take months or years, and some may never be solved.

Not all victims and witnesses are cooperative. Sometimes they do not want to be involved from the beginning of the case; other times their cooperation erodes over time. There are even those rare occasions where the victim or witness is reluctant at the beginning of the case, but becomes very cooperative as the case progresses. Additionally, victims and witnesses do not always see and remember the same thing.

Physical evidence may be missed or degrade over time. The longer it takes to discover a scene, the greater the chances of contamination, erosion, and loss of evidence. Bodies that are left in a secluded area and exposed to the elements will be compromised not only by the weather, but also by animals and insects.

Few investigators have the luxury of working one case at a time. Investigators face heavy case loads with constant pressure to clear cases. Because of these pressures, an investigator may not pursue all avenues relating to a specific case. Once there is enough information compiled to file the case, it is submitted to the District Attorney's Office and the investigator moves on to the next case.

This holds true for all investigative personnel; corporate security investigators have high case loads, in addition to having a large area to cover.

Physiological and Psychological Considerations

Conducting investigations is a physiologically and psychologically demanding job. Some investigators, depending on the investigative assignment, may spend the bulk of their careers working a specific type of investigation, while others need a change of assignment within a couple of years. This applies to all types of investigators.

Physiological considerations are evident in all investigative assignments. Investigators often work irregular hours to compile a comprehensive, professional investigation. Some investigations require extensive work over an extended period of time. Homicide detectives, defense investigators, and various types of private investigators may find themselves working twelve or fifteen hour days. If witnesses are only available on weekends or evenings, the investigator will adjust his or her work schedule to accommodate the witness.

An investigator's eating habits may also be impacted. Fast food, late hours, and little sleep often replace eating a balanced meal and taking a break from an investigation. Investigators often ingest sugars or caffeine for a quick energy boost. This can lead to weight gain, heart disease, or other physiological problems. Additionally, the round-the-clock schedule an investigation requires may impact exercise routines.

Some investigators end up working on a particular case for an extended period of time. As such, his or her leisure time is greatly impacted. Investigators must strive to maintain some type of personal time.

Although the physical aspects of the job have an impact on an investigator, the psychological aspects are often more profound and long lasting. The stress of working a case may negatively affect the investigator's mental state. Some cases require frequent travel on top of an erratic work schedule. Once off the clock, many investigators have difficulty leaving a case at work. Even when they are home, the case dominates their thoughts. This, in addition to the hectic schedule, may greatly impact an investigator's leisure or personal time.

Frequently, investigators find that law enforcement officers do not take their work seriously. They may also find that witnesses and other people who are important to the case do not wish to speak to them, for a variety of reasons. Both factors can cause additional stress for the investigator.

There is enormous pressure to close cases. The more high profile the case, the greater the pressure to solve the crime. Pressure may come from command staff, the news media, the public, and the victim's family; it may even come from the investigator himself. The investigator's response to such pressure may include erratic sleep patterns, excessive consumption of alcohol, or emotional instability, including manic behavior.

Additionally, the nature of the case itself can have a major psychological impact on the investigator. All crimes have their unique aspects, but child abuse, sexual assault, homicides, and domestic cases are more likely to negatively impact the investigator. Prolonged assignments in homicide, narcotics, or sex crimes are particularly stressful. Non-law enforcement investigations bring their own set of stressors that negatively impact the investigator.

Summary

Criminal investigators include patrol officers, lab personnel, coroner's investigators, and anyone else who contributes to the investigative process. Each of these individuals plays an important role in any investigation. Non-law enforcement investigators must possess many of the same traits found in their law enforcement counterparts. They must also be professional, provide an excellent product, and compile reports in a timely and unbiased manner.

One of the most important traits of an effective investigation is being a "people-person." Being able to relate to and empathize with people, whether they are victims, witnesses, or suspects, makes it much easier to obtain information.

Additionally, the effective investigator must know the criminal statutes and procedural law so that the results of the investigation will be admissible in court. Tied to this strong knowledge base is the thirst for knowledge. Good investigators never stop learning and asking questions.

There are several standards that come into play during the course of a criminal investigation. Law enforcement investigators must have a strong working knowledge of reasonable suspicion, probable cause, and beyond a reasonable doubt. Non-law enforcement investigators are bound by the preponderance of the evidence standard.

The majority of investigations are reactive; thus, there is a delay between the criminal act and the subsequent investigation. A major advantage of a pro-active investigation is that it is easier to control. All investigations should be treated as if a crime was committed until the investigation establishes otherwise. Once an investigation establishes that the act was non-criminal, any criminal investigation should cease.

Inductive reasoning is an essential tool of the effective investigator. Investigators use hypothetical theories when trying to determine what happened. Investigators should be flexible enough in their analysis to readily change hypothetical theories to fit the facts.

Direct evidence refers to evidence obtained from eyewitnesses who, using one or more of their five senses, obtained information relating to the crime. Circumstantial evidence is anything other than witness information and includes such things as blood spatter, DNA, dust, imprints, weapons, and questioned documents.

The investigative process takes a toll on investigators. Erratic hours, pressure to close cases, horrific details, and loss of personal time are just a few of the factors that have a negative impact on the physiological and psychological aspects of an investigator.

There is no such thing as a perfect investigation. Such factors as delay in reporting, poor initial investigation, uncooperative witnesses and victims, missed evidence, and poor documentation can have a major impact on a case.

Discussion Questions

1. You are assigned to conduct an investigation concerning a domestic violence case in which a Hispanic male assaulted his white male partner. What are the potential biases? How do you ensure those biases don't affect the investigation?

2. You are investigating a case involving an alleged sexual assault of two little girls (ages 6 and 8) by their uncle; all these parties reside in the same home. List potential direct and circumstantial evidence. As an example to get you started, interviews with the two victims would be direct evidence.

3. This Module discusses various psychological and physiological problems associated with working investigations. Discuss at least three methods you would utilize to either prevent or combat the psychological and physiological problems.

4. Research the web and find a case where the defendant was acquitted. Critique the case and discuss what was done properly and if the investigation was lacking in some respect.

Exercises

1. You are assigned to investigate a case in which a female victim alleged that while at a rock concert, an unidentified male grabbed her buttocks and then reached around her and grabbed her breasts.

   How would you conduct the initial investigation?

2. Which of the following statements are "facts," "opinions," or "conclusions?"

   Explain why a statement falls into one of these three categories.

   a. She was lying throughout the entire conversation.
   b. The amount of money taken during the bank robbery was $74300.32.
   c. Jack was sitting in the front passenger seat at the time of the accident.
   d. Since there was no forced entry into the house, the victim must have known the assailant.
   e. Males that work in day-care or pre-school positions are likely to be sex predators.

3. You are an officer working a patrol beat. You see a male that is acting "suspicious," and decide to make contact with the individual. What would you do to establish that the person was committing a crime?

Key Terms

Civil Violations: acts in violation of a law or ordinance that do not provide for an imprisonment penalty.

Continuity: an unbroken course of action moving in one continuous direction.

Criminal Investigation: an investigation into cases involving violation of criminal statutes.

Criminal Statutes: also referred to as "penal laws;" measures passed by the legislature and carry the possibility of incarceration and/or a fine.

Elements of a Crime: the necessary conditions that must exist for proof of a crime.

Evidence: anything that tends to determine or demonstrate the truth of an assertion. In court, evidence is that information (physical or verbal) that is accepted by the court to be introduced during the trial.

- **Direct Evidence:** refers to the testimony of a witness.

- **Circumstantial Evidence:** a fact that can be used to infer another fact. Examples include ballistics, DNA testing, or fingerprints.

Fact: something that is known to be true.

Feedback: the term used in the communication process to describe the process of providing re-enforcement that a person received a "message" from a person during the course of a conversation. Example: "I understand" or "I disagree with you."

Filters: factors that influence how a message is communicated.

Hypothesis: in criminal investigations, a hypothesis is an interpretation of a set of facts. The interpretation may be correct or incorrect, and is constantly being re-evaluated.

Impartial: being objective and not swayed in an opinion by bias or prejudice.

Inductive Reasoning: the type of reasoning where one draws a conclusion from a specific instance.

Inference: the drawing of a conclusion from known facts.

Initial Conclusion: a theory of the crime developed from facts immediately available at the scene.

Investigator: an individual who collects information and facts to prove or disprove an allegation.

Investigator Bias: a conflict of interest which leads an investigator to report information that is favorable to his/her theory of the case, and withhold or disregard information that contradicts that theory.

Lateral Thinking: the ability to solve problems with a creative and reasoned approach.

Opinion: a strongly held belief or position that may or may not be backed up by facts.

- **Lay opinion:** testimony from a non-expert witness that is admissible in court as long as it is rationally based on personal perception. Example: a witness to a crime testified that the suspect "seemed angry" at the scene.

- **Expert opinion:** testimony from a witness who has been accepted by the court as an expert in a relevant field.

Preponderance of Evidence: the standard that must be met for a judgment in a civil case. Preponderance means more than 51%.

Probable Cause: the standard that must be met in order before a law enforcement officer can make an arrest. To meet probable cause, there must be information that would lead a reasonable and prudent man to believe a specific person committed a specific crime.

Pro-Active Investigation: self-initiated investigations, such as setting up a controlled buy or sting operation. The investigator controls at least some of the dynamics of the offense.

Reactive Investigation: investigations in which the investigator is reacting to a crime that has already occurred.

Reasonable Suspicion: the legal standard that authorizes an officer to make contact with an individual and to detain the person for a reasonable amount of time.

Reflective Listening: a type of feedback where the listener repeats part of the message back to the sender. Example: a person tells their employer that he is not feeling well and will have to go home. The employer responds, "I am sorry to hear you are not feeling well, and agree that you should go home."

Standard of Proof: also referred to as "burden of proof." Refers to the requirements placed upon a prosecutor to prove their case.

Timeliness: to be done in an efficient and opportune manner.

Unbiased: to be free of prejudice or favoritism.

Notes

MODULE 2
Careers

Key Module Concepts:

- The basic requirements for a law enforcement career

- Non-law enforcement career paths in the criminal justice field

- State agency career opportunities

- Private investigation career options

- The similarities and differences in District Attorney's office investigator and Public Defender's office investigator positions

- The responsibilities of a forensic interviewer

- Private sector investigator positions

Introduction

When we think of an investigator, the most common image that comes to mind is of a detective that works for a law enforcement agency. After all, according to the 2008 Bureau of Labor Statistics, there were 883,600 police and detective jobs in the United States. Of those, approximately 79% of those positions were with local government agencies and 11% with state law enforcement agencies.

However, investigation-related careers are not limited to law enforcement. Some individuals enjoy the prospect of conducting investigations, but are not drawn to the law enforcement environment. The following is a brief discussion of some of the investigation-oriented opportunities available both in law enforcement and non-law enforcement fields. Since many of the specific requirements vary from state to state, the provided information is offered as a starting point only.

Most investigator positions require some degree of experience and education. New hires in law enforcement usually have to spend several years working patrol before applying for an investigator position. This may vary depending on the size or specific needs of a department.

Here are some points to keep in mind when checking out potential career paths associated with investigations:

- Many law enforcement candidates start their careers in small departments or one type of agency and change departments or types of agencies several times throughout their careers

- A number of non-law enforcement investigator positions don't require the candidate to have prior law enforcement experience

- Many law enforcement departments have a **ride-along program** in which individuals can ride with a patrol officer during his shift. This is a practical means of understanding what a law enforcement officer's job entails. Some agencies also offer internships, which provide additional insight into law enforcement as a possible career.

The following discussion centers on the most common investigative positions. Since the requirements may vary from agency to agency, contact should be made with the specific agency to learn what activities and requirements are relevant to the position.

Ask Yourself

- *What are the requirements to be a law enforcement investigator?*
- *What are the requirements to be a private investigator?*
- *What are the possible career choices involving investigations?*

Investigative Agencies

Police/Sheriff Agencies

Potential law enforcement investigators must determine what type of agency they want to work for. Options for employment include police departments, sheriff's offices, federal agencies, and college campus police departments. They must also decide whether they would prefer working for a large, mid-sized, or small department. Each option has positive and negative aspects. Large departments have more career opportunities, but the competition for those positions is very strong. It may be easier to move into an investigator position in a small department, but the smaller agencies do not have the variety of cases or assignments associated with larger departments.

Police departments enforce the law on a city/municipal level. The chief of police is usually an appointed position. It is not uncommon for the chief of a large department to hold that position for many years.

Traditionally, an individual would join a police or sheriff's department and work in a patrol or detentions assignment for six months to a year, depending on the agency's requirements.

After that period of time, the officer could apply for a transfer to investigations. At one time, in large metropolitan areas, competition for investigator positions was very high. Investigator positions were held in high esteem, and there was a pay increase because many departments saw the transfer as a promotion.

The situation has changed somewhat. Today, the competition for detective positions may not be as high as it was in earlier times. Many people value their time away from work and are not interested in a position that requires being on-call outside of designated work hours, making court appearances, or carrying a heavy case load. Many other assignments in law enforcement, such as patrol, have limited overtime and no **on-call** requirement. Today it is not uncommon to see candidates with one or two years experience assigned to a detective bureau. In some police departments, investigators are assigned to cases for an indeterminate period of time. In other departments, officers assigned to investigations will rotate into other departments after a couple of years.

Sheriff's departments enforce the law at the county level. Sheriffs are usually elected officials and are, in most jurisdictions, responsible for the operation of the county jail. As such, there are career opportunities in detention centers that are not available in police departments.

Many sheriff's departments require that new hires spend a minimum of six months working in the detention section of the department before competing for patrol/investigations assignments.

Sheriff's departments have investigative units, and the larger departments have specialized units within the investigations section. As with police departments, sheriff's departments may rotate their investigators after a couple of years or allow them to remain in their assignment for an indeterminate amount of time.

State Police and State Patrol are state law enforcement agencies. State Patrol is responsible for the enforcement of motor vehicle laws and regulations, and for investigation of traffic accidents on state highways. State Police agencies, which do not exist in all states, have the responsibility of conducting criminal investigations in addition to their motor vehicle violation and accident responsibilities.

State investigator positions may have an education and experience requirement. More state agencies are requiring that criminal investigators hold a POST certification (or similar certification earned through the state). POST stands for Police Officer Standard of Training, and is required only if the investigator is going to make arrests. To obtain POST certification a candidate must either

- Be hired by a law enforcement agency and attend the agency's academy. Once the candidate has successfully completed the academy, the agency files the appropriate paperwork with the State.

- Attend a POST certification academy. Candidates in this academy have not been hired by an agency, or the agency that hired them is not large enough to conduct its own academy. Candidates who successfully complete the academy, but aren't already hired by a law enforcement agency, will be "POST certifiable," meaning that when an agency hires the candidate, he or she will be certified as a police officer in that state.

If the candidate has prior police experience in another state, or his POST certification has expired, the candidate can take a written test and demonstrate proficiency in the areas of arrest techniques, firearm proficiency, and defensive driving.

Each state has investigators who work **administrative investigations**, such as **regulatory violation** cases, which include state licensing, bail bonds, securities, and workers' compensation. If the investigation results in the detection of potential criminal acts, the investigator may conduct the entire inquiry before referring it to a criminal investigator on behalf of the Attorney General's Office. Administrative investigators work case files, conduct interviews, and perform the function of a criminal investigator, minus having the authority to make arrests. They do not have the authority to make arrests, and are not required to have POST certification. Candidates are processed through the state's hiring process and are evaluated on their education and experience. State agencies that might employ criminal and/or administrative investigators include:

- Department of Social Services
- Attorney General's Office
- Department of Insurance
- Department of Securities
- Department of Revenue
- Department of Real Estate
- Department of Corrections: Youth Services

Unlike administrative investigators, Department of Corrections investigators are usually authorized to make arrests. They conduct investigations concerning alleged criminal violations by inmates within the state prison system. Depending on the state, Department of Corrections investigators may also investigate other alleged crimes associated with law enforcement personnel.

Some police and sheriff's departments allow candidates to apply with a high school degree, or a G.E.D., as long as the candidate is over eighteen, with no criminal record, is a U.S. citizen, and is drug free. Some departments do require a college degree. The candidate applies directly through the local sheriff's office or police department for openings within that agency. The application process includes a written examination, physical fitness evaluation, an oral board, background check, and a psychological exam. Some agencies require that the candidates take a polygraph examination as well.

Once an applicant has completed all of these phases, the applicant is placed on an "eligibility list" and ranked according to the cumulative scores of the various phases. Individuals who are hired from the eligibility list go through either a residential or day academy that ranges from between twelve and fifteen weeks, depending on the agency.

FIGURE 2.1: *There are many options for investigators who wish to work for the federal government.*

Federal Investigative Positions

There are numerous federal investigator positions that enforce specific types of laws. For instance, the Federal Bureau of Investigation (F.B.I.) is responsible for the investigation of more than 200 categories of federal law. Like their state counterparts, FBI agents may conduct surveillance, investigate white-collar crimes, and testify in court. The FBI has a criminal profiling unit, and also looks into offenses such as organized crime, racketeering, public corruption, bank robbery, kidnapping, and cyber crime.

Other federal agencies enforce specific laws. The U.S. Drug Enforcement Administration (DEA) enforces laws relating to illegal drugs. U.S. Marshals provide witness protection concerning federal cases, and provides security for federal courts. The Bureau of Alcohol, Tobacco, Firearms, and Explosives investigate violations of federal firearms and explosives laws. In addition to providing protection for the President, the Secret Service investigates forgery and counterfeiting cases. Other federal agencies that employ investigators are the Postal Service, the Bureau of Indian Affairs, the Department of Agriculture, Homeland Security, and Border Patrol.

Applying for a position with a federal law enforcement agency requires a college degree and an extensive hiring process. The competition for these positions is intense and time consuming. Although it is possible for an individual to go into a federal law enforcement agency immediately after obtaining a college degree, a large number of the new hires are individuals who have some law enforcement experience in addition to a degree. Depending on the agency, a candidate with a degree in a specialized area such as law, accounting, or forensic sociology may have an advantage over other applicants. Applicants who are accepted by the FBI attend a seventeen-week long academy at Quantico. Other federal agencies' academies vary in length and location. Once training is completed, agents receive their first field assignments, which may be anywhere in the United States.

District Attorney's Office Investigators

Unlike law enforcement agencies, there is no uniformity as to the structure, supervision hierarchy, or role of an investigative unit with a District Attorney's (D.A.) office. In fact, not all District Attorney offices have investigators. In some offices all investigators are commissioned law enforcement officers, while other offices have investigators who are not commissioned law enforcement officers. Some offices have a chief investigator, while in other offices the investigators are under the supervision of a Chief Deputy District Attorney.

The primary role of an investigator in a District Attorney's office is to provide **court support**, or to assist the D.A.'s office while preparing for trial. After a case has been filed with the District Attorney's office, the assigned deputy District Attorney often determines what additional investigation is needed prior to trial. In some instances, the investigator who filed the criminal charges will conduct the additional investigation, but it is not uncommon for the D.A.'s office investigator to conduct a follow-up investigation. Additionally, the investigator may be requested to conduct pro-active investigations, serve subpoenas, locate witnesses, and assist the deputy D.A. with pre-trial interviews. Some D.A.'s offices have specialized units, such as Family Violence, Check Fraud, or Economic Crime. The units are usually comprised of a Chief Deputy D.A., Deputy D.A.s, investigators, and victim advocates.

There are no uniform application requirements or testing procedures. Some offices go through a civil service type application process, while other offices only conduct interviews of candidates who apply directly to the office.

While most District Attorneys' offices hire investigators with law enforcement background, some offices offer positions that do not require prior experience. Since there is no uniformity as to the composition of the investigative units or requirements for employment, candidates should contact the District Attorney's office they are considering and inquire as to job responsibilities and qualification requirements.

Once the new investigator is hired, he must complete a probationary period. Many newly hired investigators will be assigned to court support in a specific courtroom. After a couple of years, the investigator may be re-assigned to one of the specialized units within the office.

Investigators with previous law enforcement experience may have trouble transitioning into a District Attorney's office. The District Attorney's office is primarily a law office, and an investigator may be seen as part of the support staff. While investigators are still treated with respect and often enjoy good working relationships with attorneys, the dynamics are markedly different than working in a law enforcement agency.

Public Defender's Office Investigators

The role of an investigator in the Public Defender's office is similar to that of the investigator for the District Attorney, with two major differences: Public Defender's office investigators do not have law enforcement authority, and their investigation is on behalf of the defendant. Like their District Attorney's office counterparts, these investigators conduct interviews, assist attorneys in the evaluation of cases, collect evidence, and sometimes testify in court. They may also be required to find witnesses and serve subpoenas. However, Public Defender investigators face markedly different challenges than their District Attorney's office counterparts. Victims and witnesses for the prosecution may be disinclined to speak with them and law enforcement officers don't see them in the same light as law enforcement investigators.

These investigators may have previous law enforcement experience or private investigations experience. In some jurisdictions, candidates with little investigative experience may be hired, especially if the candidate has good analytical and writing skills.

Like their District Attorney's office counterparts, Public Defender's office investigators must be able to critically analyze a case, interact with a wide range of audiences, and write concise and timely reports.

Most Public Defender's offices require that a newly hired investigator complete a probationary period. As with their District Attorney's office counterparts, the Public Defender's investigators often start off working court support, but may work themselves into more specialized assignments.

Public Defender's office investigator positions are available at the county and federal levels. Investigators for the federal Public Defender's office assist in the investigation and case preparation for federal cases. Public Defender's office investigators are government employees, with all of the benefits of their District Attorney's office counterparts.

Training opportunities for this position vary from state to state. Individuals who do not have law enforcement experience may be viable candidates if they have a two or four year degree in criminal justice or one of the social sciences. The Criminal Defense Investigation Training Counsel provides training and educational programs for potential and established Public Defender's Office investigators.

Forensic Interviewer

The primary role of a forensic interviewer is to conduct legally sound and objective interviews of victims. Emphasis is on the use of non-leading interviewing techniques and detailed documentation of the information obtained from the victim or witness. The forensic interview often occurs shortly after allegations of sexual abuse or physical abuse are reported. The interviews are video and audio-recorded to reduce the number of times a victim is interviewed. Forensic interviewers are often required to testify in criminal cases.

They are most often subpoenaed by the prosecution and are used to admit the interview into evidence.

The Center for Interviewer Standards (CISA) requires a high school diploma and a minimum of two years' experience conducting investigations in either the public or private sector. The candidate must also take the Certified Forensic Investigator Examination. The examination covers topics that include interviewing techniques, legal aspects of interviewing, interview setting, false confessions, and fact gathering. Once the candidate has successfully passed the Certified Forensic Investigator Examination, the candidate must be re-certified every three years.

Although most forensic interviewer positions are associated with the Department of Social Services and Advocacy Centers, some private corporations employ forensic interviewers in their loss prevention programs.

FIGURE 2.2: *The private sector has much to offer an open-minded investigator.*

Private Industry

Private industry utilizes investigators for a variety of purposes. Some investigators look into thefts at the work place, provide a safe work environment, and provide security. Insurance investigators explore **insurer fraud**, which includes fraud by employees of the insurance industry. They also investigate **insurance fraud**, which is the generic term for fraud by policyholders and individuals filing claims against an insurance carrier.

Some insurance and commercial entities have security investigators, who conduct investigations that affect the corporation. Cases could involve embezzlement, theft, workplace violence, and trade secret violations. While many of these investigators have law enforcement backgrounds, some positions are held by long-term employees who know the workings of the company.

Private security companies, whose primary function is to protect **corporate assets** (possessions of a business) may have security and patrol functions. These companies are non-law enforcement and therefore have no POST certification requirement.

Retail loss prevention also centers on protection of assets, but on a different level than private security companies. The focus here is on shoplifting, credit card fraud and **shrinkage** (loss of product due to theft, loss or contamination). These are non-law enforcement positions, and entry-level positions are available, usually as store security. There is potential for professional development in this area and it is a viable lead to law enforcement positions.

Loss prevention training is often offered by the employer to fulfill in-house needs. The Loss Prevention Foundation also offers on-line certification courses. There is no educational or prior law enforcement experience requirement for this position.

Private Investigators

Private investigators are often hired by attorneys to assist in cases, by corporations to conduct investigations when the corporation either doesn't have the personnel to handle the investigation or because of a confidentiality aspect, or by individuals who need the services of an investigator. Some private investigators specialize in areas such as private security, criminal cases, divorce cases, or insurance fraud.

As with any investigator position, the private investigator has to be detail oriented and possess excellent and effective communication skills. Unlike a law enforcement officer who has access to a wide range of databases and a strong network of law enforcement agencies, the private investigator often relies on his skills and a communication network that he establishes on his own. Private investigators are dependent upon knowing where and how to access various databases. They are often experts in finding background information in this fashion, since they cannot rely upon search warrants to obtain necessary information.

Surveillance is commonly associated with private investigation. An insurance agency may want to determine if an insured is faking a worker's compensation claim. A civil attorney may need information to determine if a person has enough assets before deciding to sue. A corporate executive wants a low-profile investigation to ascertain if one of the company's high executives has a drinking or gambling problem. Placing the parties under surveillance can lead to quicker resolution of these issues.

Private investigators, along with corporate investigators, insurance investigators and security companies, may also work in an area that has high exposure for businesses: industrial accidents. Could a given accident have been avoided? Was the accident a result of faulty equipment or hazardous work conditions? Is the company responsible, or liable, for the accident?

Example

A cooling tower for a power plant collapsed, killing 51 construction workers. The cause of the collapse was determined to be a result of placing loads on recently poured concrete before it was cured, causing the concrete to collapse. Private investigators may interview vendors, construction workers and supervisors to ascertain if corners were cut during construction, or if the company used poor grade materials to increase profits. Such information could be critical in a civil suit against the contractor.

Such situations require in-depth investigations into what caused the disaster and into the resulting damages. The investigation may result in multiple civil suits and potential criminal filings. Litigation in such cases can go on for years.

Private investigators must be knowledgeable about the law. Although they do not have to worry about Fourth Amendment issues, they must be cognitive of various legal issues, such as privacy law. They also do not have the same type of immunity or protection afforded law enforcement officers. For instance, if a private investigator seizes evidence, it may be admissible in court, but depending on how the evidence was obtained, the investigator may be subject to arrest for trespassing or theft.

Since some states don't require any licensing or minimum standards, anyone can become a private investigator. There are several different employment options; private investigators may work (either as an employee or as a contractor) for another PI or for an agency. However, almost a fourth of all private investigators are self-employed, and they often compete in a limited market. The individual who goes directly into private investigations without previous experience often competes against retired police detectives and retired federal law enforcement agents for jobs. Unless a private investigator has a "niche market," meaning that they bring a unique ability or expertise to the table, private investigator jobs are often obtained because of the employing agency's reputation or because they have established contacts during their law enforcement careers. A private investigator's work hours are often irregular and may be sporadic; he often works alone, without backup. Should he decide that he needs a gun, he must obtain a concealed weapon permit.

Private investigation agencies are private businesses, and there is no uniformity in hiring procedure or criteria. Some firms will hire candidates who do not have any investigative experience for surveillance and research purposes.

Many private investigators have attended college and/or have law enforcement experience. Private investigators who specialize in white-collar crimes, such as computer crime and corporate espionage, can demand high fees. Other services performed by private investigators include personal security, process service, witness location, or compiling information for civil or criminal cases; he or she will receive significantly smaller fees for these services. Having consistent work and getting paid are often cited as major problems for the private investigator.

Knowledge of (and background in) computer forensics, accounting, and computer science are of great benefit to the private investigator. Many investigators take classes on such topics as surveillance, photography, statement taking, and investigative techniques. ASIS International, a trade organization in the security industry, offers a "Professional Certified Investigator" certification. The National Association of Legal Investigators also offers programs and certifications.

Liability Issues

All investigators face liability, or financial responsibility, when they are responsible for actions including assault and battery, libel, slander, and false arrest. Law enforcement investigators have liability insurance coverage through the city, county, or state agency that hired them. Private investigators and security companies, however, must obtain their own liability insurance, including **Errors and Omissions Insurance**, which protects from claims that the investigator or the company made an error or failed to perform as promised in a contract.

Comparing and Contrasting Law Enforcement and Non-Law Enforcement Career Paths

Law enforcement careers and non-law enforcement careers both have many advantages and disadvantages. Law enforcement jobs have traditionally been seen as secure, with few layoffs or cuts. While salaries may not be as high as some private positions, most departments have a good retirement package, insurance coverage, and a set structure regarding command and expectations.

While many private companies or agencies in the private sector pride themselves on providing an outstanding product or service, they are also concerned about making a profit. If revenues are down, there may be reduction in staff. If a market gets saturated with too many vendors, companies may fold or be purchased by another company who has their own investigations staff. This can happen to small or large companies.

Law enforcement officers are provided standardized training and the means of developing and maintaining proficiencies in various areas associated with their jobs. They attend an academy, receive in-service training, and are afforded career-advancing opportunities. There is no uniformity of training for non-law enforcement investigators. Their level of training often depends on what the agency deems important or is more economical.

In many ways, a law enforcement investigator's function is well defined. He can make arrests under certain conditions, has the authority to obtain warrants and is authorized to use deadly force in certain circumstances. As long as the criteria are met, the officer will be afforded protection in the performance of his duties. The private investigator's activities are not as clearly defined, nor is he afforded the same protections as a police officer.

Private investigators enjoy more freedom than their law enforcement counterparts. A law enforcement investigator cannot pick and choose what crimes he is going to investigate. Private investigators can take or refuse a case without any ramifications.

Partial List of Other Potential Investigator Positions:

- Airport Security
- Animal Control Officer
- Bailiffs
- Border Patrol
- Bounty Hunter
- Coroner's Investigator
- Criminologist
- Compliance Officer
- Corrections Officer
- Court Reporters
- Fire Investigators
- Fish and Game
- Forensic Toxicologist
- Fraud Examiner
- Homeland Security
- Paralegal
- Parks Ranger
- Security

FIGURE 2.3: *Investigators may provide airport security for a number of situations.*

Example

Jack Smith is accused of a criminal act. A police department detective conducts an investigation and files the case against Smith with the District Attorney's (D.A.'s) office. Once the case is filed, the D.A. assigns an office investigator to conduct follow-up interviews and subpoenas the witnesses for trial in order to prove his case against Smith.

Smith initially had a Public Defender (PD) represent him. The PD assigns one of her investigators to attempt to locate alibi witnesses and subpoena witnesses for Smith. Smith then obtains money to retain a private defense attorney, who hires a private investigator to look into the case. The information that the private investigator uncovers is turned over to the defense attorney to be used in trial. Because of his extensive investigative background, the defense attorney subpoenas the private investigator to talk about crime scene contamination and interviewing techniques in an attempt to discredit the investigation done by the law enforcement detective.

Summary

There are many opportunities for investigative careers, both inside and outside law enforcement. The competition for any investigator position is very high. The individual just getting into the investigative field faces competition from those with law enforcement or private investigative experience.

For those going into private investigations, the competition is even greater. Many private investigative agencies are comprised of former law enforcement investigators who have established a good reputation while working in the criminal justice system and have a strong network that facilitates getting work. The private sector expects a quality product for its money, thus they are very discriminating in their choice of private investigative firms.

Government positions provide job security, paid benefits, and a set structure. While some private industry positions may not have the same degree of job security, they may provide higher salary and more flexibility as to what work is done and how it is done. As is the case with private investigative agencies, corporate positions are often filled with individuals with previous law enforcement experience or retired federal investigators.

Neither law enforcement nor private investigations is as glamorous as portrayed on television. Both positions require a great deal of hard work, long hours, and a great deal of stress. Any investigator may spend hours with little activity; followed by a period of time of great activity. A private investigator has the added stress of looking for work, covering expenses, and making a profit so that he can stay in business.

Investigative positions, be it law enforcement or private, provide a great deal of challenges and rewards. The work is very gratifying and each day brings new challenges. It is also not uncommon for people to periodically change investigative positions throughout their career. An individual may start out as a patrol officer, become a detective, take a **corporate security** position, and then become a private investigator.

Discussion Questions

1. How does a District Attorney's office investigator's role differ from that of a law enforcement investigator's role? How are they similar?

2. How does a corporate investigator's role differ from that of a law enforcement investigator's role? How are they similar?

3. Should there be standardized requirements and licensing for private investigators?

4. Discuss the various career opportunities available to individuals who don't want to be a law enforcement investigator.

5. Discuss the pros and cons of being a private investigator.

Exercises

1. Using the Internet, research the requirements for both a local sheriff's office and police department.
   a. What, if any, are the differences in the basic requirements for application?
   b. Is there a significant difference in salaries between the two agencies?
   c. Did the sheriff's office require new employees to work in detentions prior to going to the streets?

2. Using the Internet, research the requirements for being a private investigator in your state.
   a. Does your state require that a private investigator be licensed?
   b. Is there any testing or classes that must be completed prior to obtaining a license?
   c. Are private investigators required to be bonded in your state?
   d. What is the starting salary for an entry-level private investigator at an agency?

3. Using the Internet and contacting the local Public Defender's office, find out the following information:
   a. What are the education and experience requirements to be a Public Defender's office investigator?
   b. What are the primary duties of a Public Defender's office investigator?
   c. What is the salary of a Public Defender's office investigator? How does it compared to the salaries earned by a law enforcement officer or a private investigator?

4. After obtaining the information for the first three exercises, compare and contrast the pros and cons of these career options.

Resources

To find federal, state, and local law enforcement job fairs and other recruiting events:

National Law Enforcement Recruiters Association
P.O. Box 17132
Arlington, VA 22216
(703) 528-5600
http://www.nlera.org

For general information about sheriffs and to learn more about National Sheriffs' Association Scholarships:

National Sheriffs' Association
1450 Duke St.,
Alexandria, VA 22314
(703) 836-7827
(800) 424-7827 (Toll Free)
http://www.sheriffs.org

For information about chiefs of police:

International Association of Chiefs of Police
515 N. Washington St.,
Alexandria, VA 22314
(703) 836-6767
(800) THE-IACP (Toll Free)
http://www.theiacp.org

Information about qualifications for employment as a Federal Bureau of Investigation (FBI) Special Agent is available from the nearest State FBI office. The address and phone number are listed in the local telephone directory. The FBI can be found on the Internet at:
http://www.fbi.gov

Information on career opportunities, qualifications, and training for U.S. Secret Service Special Agents and Uniformed Officers:

U.S. Secret Services
Recruitment and Hiring Coordination Center
245 Murray Dr., Building 410
Washington, DC 20223
(202) 406-5830 (Recruitment Program)
(202) 406-5458 (Applicant Information and Assistance)
http://www.secretservice.gov/join

Information about employment as a Drug Enforcement Administration (DEA) Special Agent:

Drug Enforcement Administration
Office of Personnel
8701 Morrissette Dr.,
Springfield, VA 22152
(800) DEA-4288
http://www.usdoj.gov/dea

Information about jobs in other Federal Law Enforcement Agencies:

U.S. Marshals Service
Human Resources Division: Recruitment
Washington, DC 20530-1000
(202) 616-0682
http://www.usmarshals.gov

U.S. Bureau of Alcohol, Tobacco, Firearms and Explosives
Recruitment, Hiring and Staffing Center
99 New York Ave. NE
Washington, DC 20226
(202) 648-9100
http://www.atf.gov

U.S. Customs and Border Protection
1300 Pennsylvania Ave. NW
Washington, DC 20229
http://www.cbp.gov

U.S. Department of Homeland Security
245 Murray Drive SW, Building 410
Washington, DC 20528
http://www.dhs.gov

Key Terms

Administrative Investigations: cases that involve regulatory violations, such as state licensing, bail bonds, securities, and workers' compensation.

Corporate Assets: refers to the items that are owned or controlled by a corporation.

Corporate Security: may involve the physical security of the corporation's buildings and/or the investigation of cases involving the corporation's assets, such as theft and embezzlement.

Court Support: refers to the investigative function of assisting the District Attorney or Public Defender's Offices in preparing a case for trial.

Errors and Omissions Insurance: business liability insurance that covers errors or omissions on the part of a company that may cause financial harm to someone else.

Insurance Fraud: deception committed by insurance policy holders against an insurance company for unfair gain.

Insurer Fraud: deception that is committed by an employee or agent of an insurance company.

Liability: the obligation to pay a debt in response to an action.

On-Call: being available to work outside designated hours.
POST Certification: credential that signifies the officer has completed the peace officer's standard of training for that state and is a certified police officer.

Regulatory Violations: violations of state statutes that normally involve a fine or licensing sanction; but do not involve incarceration.

Ride-along Program: a program that allows citizens to ride with a patrol officer during the officer's shift.

Shrinkage: a business term that refers to the loss of product via theft, loss, or contamination.

Notes

MODULE 3

Preliminary Response

Key Module Concepts:

- The immediate responsibilities an officer has when responding to a crime scene

- Inner and outer crime scene perimeters

- How contamination may occur during the initial investigation of a case

- Why traditional interviews are used in an initial investigation

- The three most common forms of documentation used during the initial investigation of a crime

Introduction

Although this Module applies primarily to law enforcement, it also has practical applications for other investigators. What is done in the initial investigation, or the preliminary response, has a major impact on any subsequent investigation. The initial investigation sets the stage for the follow-up investigation. Things done correctly to ensure an effective investigation. When things are done poorly, or incorrectly, the investigation suffers.

It is important that people in all investigation-related careers have a strong working knowledge of the dynamics associated with the initial response. District Attorney office investigators often assist in the follow-up investigation and prepare the case for trial. Public Defender's office investigators examine and evaluate what occurred during the initial investigation and try to poke holes in the prosecution's case, while private investigators may use information obtained during the initial investigation to conduct their follow-up investigation. Private investigators conduct follow-up investigations based upon the information obtained during the initial investigation. Sometimes corporate security investigators or private security officers are the first responders to a crime and utilize the same techniques used by law enforcement in conducting initial investigations.

The steps listed in this Module can be applied to investigations of both violent crimes, such as homicides, robberies, sexual assaults, serious bodily injury assaults, and property crimes such as theft, embezzlement, and burglary.

Ask Yourself

- *What needs to be done during the initial investigation?*
- *What is contamination and how do you avoid it?*
- *What are the various types of interviews?*

Initial Response

Most investigations begin with a 911 call or a citizen's call for assistance. Someone such as an uninvolved person, a witness, a victim, or even the suspect, calls and talks to a 911 operator or a law enforcement agency dispatcher. The dispatcher obtains general information from the caller. Officers are then dispatched to the scene. The dispatcher attempts to get as much information from the caller as possible to assist responding officers, as well as any fire personnel and paramedics that might be needed at the scene. In addition to getting names, addresses, victim and suspect information and details on the nature of the crime, the dispatcher attempts to get the caller calm and focused. This may be difficult, as 911 calls can be emotionally charged. The caller may be confused, frightened, injured, or some combination of all three. Depending on the nature of the call, the dispatcher may also talk to the fire department and paramedics, who will also be responding to the scene. All this initial information is critical for the responding officers, paramedics, and fire personnel.

Even with the outstanding job dispatchers do on a routine basis, responding officers may not have a complete picture of the situation they are responding to. As we discussed in Module One, some filtering of information occurs during stressful situations, whether from the caller, from the dispatcher to the responding officers, and even among the officers responding to the scene.

FIGURE 3.1: *The way investigators respond to the scene can set the tone for the entire investigation.*

Responding Officer Dynamics

Responding to the scene is one of the most emotional aspects of the job. In addition to obtaining as much accurate information as possible from dispatch, the responding officers have additional responsibilities and distractions. Officers often respond to the scene with sirens and red, flashing lights; this is called running code. Although this appears to be an exciting aspect of the job, running code doesn't relieve the officer of his responsibility for the safety of other drivers or of any civil liability. Additionally, turning on the lights and sirens has a psychological and physiological impact on the officer. Adrenaline increases, heart rate accelerates, and the mind races. Coupled with these dynamics are the additional responsibilities of getting to the scene as quickly as possible, coordinating with other responding officers, and formulating a plan based upon the information available at the time.

The officer may experience "tunnel vision," focusing on getting to the scene to help ensure the scene isn't contaminated. Tunnel vision may cause the responding officers to not notice potential witnesses, vehicles, or even the suspect. Since no two people will react the same way, the effects of these dynamics may vary from officer to officer, but they always exist to some degree. Other factors, such as lack of sleep, financial difficulties, relationship issues, and other obligations may be on an investigator's mind. It is important to always bring your "A-game."

As the officers approach the scene, one officer is usually designated to lead the response. It is that officer's responsibility to coordinate the approach to the scene, establish a crime scene perimeter, give preliminary assignments, and ensure the safety of people and preserve the crime scene.

Arrive Safely

The priorities of initial responders are to arrive at the scene safely, make the scene safe, render aid, and preserve the crime scene. It is critical that the officers arrive safely at the scene. If an officer gets involved in an accident, the impact is greater than the officer's absence. An officer-involved accident will require the response of a supervisor and other patrol officers. Officers from other areas will have to be assigned to the initial call. If the officer's accident involves injuries, paramedics and fire department personnel would also be impacted.

Make the Scene Safe/Rendering Aid

Once the officers arrive safely at the scene, their first priority is to make sure the scene is safe and render aid. **Making the scene safe** means dealing with any potential threat and ensuring that no other people are in danger. Once the scene is deemed safe, the officers render aid to any injured parties. Some situations require that the initial responders wait for assistance. A barricaded suspect, a potential bomb situation, or a bank robbery in progress may prevent officers from taking immediate action, as that may cause more casualties.

FIGURE 3.2: *Investigators must take care that the crime scene is not compromised or contaminated.*

Preserving the Crime Scene

After any potential threat has been addressed and victims have been tended to, the officer turns his attention to preserving the crime scene. Preserving the crime scene is essential. It is important to keep in mind that any crime scene is constantly subject to contamination, meaning that evidence may be compromised, lost or destroyed. Witnesses may leave the scene or talk to other witnesses. If the suspect is on scene and is combative, the scene may be compromised. If paramedics render aid to people at the scene, their actions may result in furniture being moved, destroyed evidence, or discarded medical paraphernalia left in the crime scene. Bodies may be moved and clothing removed in an effort to render aid.

The first step in preserving the scene is establishing inner and outer perimeters. Depending on the nature of the case, an outer perimeter may be the same as the inner perimeter. The **inner perimeter** is that area that includes the crime scene and those areas associated with the crime. Establishing the inner perimeter may be a challenge, as the initial officers may not know the magnitude of the case; for instance, whether everything occurred within one room of a residence, or if there were multiple incidents in multiple locations. Crime scenes are also a challenge in that every scene is different. The rule of thumb is that a crime scene perimeter can be reduced, but not expanded. When in doubt, make your perimeter larger than it needs to be. For example, if part of the crime occurred inside a house, but then continued onto the street, the inner perimeter should potentially include the entire block.

The **outer perimeter** is the staging area for non-law enforcement personnel. Depending on the crime, news media, onlookers, and members of the victim's family may be present. Placing them in the outer perimeter ensures that they won't contaminate the scene, but are still afforded some access. Once the crime scene has been secured, a point of entry into the scene must be established. The point of entry is manned by an officer who does not allow anyone into the scene without signing in on the crime scene log. Most departments adhere to the policy that anyone entering a crime scene is responsible for writing a report addressing what he or she did while in the scene. Once the scene has been made safe and the victim(s) are treated, no one should be in the scene until either consent or a search warrant is obtained to conduct the investigation.

Entering the Scene

An investigator's job is to conduct a thorough, yet timely, investigation that helps lead to the arrest of the guilty and the exoneration of the innocent. One of the most critical aspects of an investigation deals with the lawful entry and seizing of evidence. For our purposes, we will assume that the investigator has either obtained a search warrant or consent to enter the crime scene.

Before entering the scene, the investigator should get into a routine that includes the following:

- Sign the crime scene log (see Exhibit A in Resources)

- Put on gloves

- Take out a pen and notebook, and start observing. Take in the whole scene, not only the most interesting or most obvious factors. What is out of place? What is missing? How did the suspect enter and exit the scene? Don't start hypothesizing before you get all the facts.

Remember: Don't make the facts fit your hypothesis; have your hypothesis fit your facts.

Example

Dispatch advises a patrol officer of an "assault in progress" call.

Dispatch provides the officer with the address, information concerning the call, and any history pertaining to the address.

While receiving this information from dispatch, the officer determines where the address is, the quickest way to get to the address, and whether or not to respond to the scene with red lights and sirens.

Other officers are also on the air and responding to the call. The primary officer is thinking about what he has to do when he gets to the scene and what he will need of the other officers. The officer is also thinking of what may be at the scene when he arrives, such as injured parties, armed suspects, number of people at the scene, and preserving evidence.

The officer arrives in the area of the scene, and parks a few houses away from the actual address. Getting out of his car, the officer takes in all of the sounds and sights in the area. As he approaches the scene, the officer is thinking about the type of call, looking for signs of potential problems, and how to best approach the house.

Once contact is made with the residents, the officer is concerned about officer safety, ascertaining if anyone is injured, making sure no potential threats exist, and ascertaining what occurred. When the officer determines that the scene is safe, no one is injured, and there are no threats, he determines if a crime occurred, should he make an arrest, and preserve any evidence.

Conducting searches inside a residence require a systematic approach, ensuring that all areas to be searched are covered. Searching the interior of a building should only be done when the officer(s) can do so safely. Exterior searches have their own unique challenges are usually conducted in one of three manners: Lane,

Circle, or Zone/Sector:

- **Lane:** Divide the area into lanes, using stakes and a string. An officer is assigned to each lane and each searches the area within his lane. The lanes may not always be staked out. Sometimes officers will walk "shoulder-to-shoulder," looking at the area within their lane of travel.

- **Circle:** The search begins at the center of an area and spreads out in an ever-widening concentric circle pattern. This activity continues until the entire area is covered.

- **Zone/Sector:** The area to be searched is divided into equal squares on a map of the area to be searched and each square is given a number. An officer is assigned a number and is responsible for searching that zone.

Contamination of Evidence

Contamination of evidence is foremost in an investigator's mind. Critical evidence could be lost if evidence is not handled properly. Fingerprints can be obliterated, DNA samples destroyed, footprints ruined. To lower the chance of evidence contamination, the only people touching anything at the scene should be investigators who are collecting evidence. Likewise, investigators should not use anything at the scene (toilet, sink, or phone), as these items may contain evidence that is critical to the case.

An investigator can also contaminate information received from witnesses, victims or suspects. How victims and witnesses are dealt with, the types of questions they are asked, and where the questioning occurs can hinder individuals from providing complete and accurate information, thus handicapping investigators' search for the truth. Potential contamination, as it relates to interviews conducted in the initial investigation, takes two forms: investigator-initiated and witness-initiated.

Investigator-initiated contamination centers on the interview process. The interviewing technique used during the initial phase of an investigation is markedly different from the interview technique used in the follow-up phase of the investigation. During the initial phase, officers and investigators use the **traditional technique** that emphasizes obtaining pertinent information quickly. The traditional technique is often characterized by using **closed-ended questions**, which require either a "yes" or "no" answer or short responses. Traditional technique questioning centers on the "5 Ws and How" questions (Who, What, When, Where, Why and How). Examples are: "Who did this?" "What did he do?" Where is he now?" When did this happen?" "Why did he attack you?" "How did this happen?"

The traditional technique is very effective in the initial investigation, when responders are attempting to obtain a quick assessment of the situation, or are working to get suspect information out to other officers. Additionally, information obtained during this phase from the victim, witnesses, and the suspect will often have a direct bearing on the success of the investigation. Many situations are emotionally charged and the interviewee is not in the frame of mind to provide a full narrative of what happened. Quick, short questions are very effective in these situations. The downside is that there is a great potential for contamination of information. Failing to build rapport, or being perceived as inconsiderate or officious, can negatively impact the information a person will readily provide. While the traditional technique provides quick information, it runs a greater risk of being contaminated. For example: The officer asks a witness, "Did you see the red car?" If the witness thought they saw a blue car, they may decide they were wrong in their observation and tell the officer that they saw a red car.

Witness-Initiated Contamination

Another source of contamination during this phase, called **witness-initiated contamination**, deals with information being shared among witnesses. If witnesses are allowed to be together, they may compare their observations with each other. When that occurs, witness observations may change, or at least be influenced by the information received from other witnesses. Because of this contamination risk, all witnesses should be separated from one another until they can be interviewed.

Initial Interview of Victims and Possible Contamination

In some situations, victims can be considered a witness to the crime, as they may have to testify in court about the events that occurred. However, victims sometimes have no recall of the crime and in that regard cannot be considered witnesses. Interviewing victims to establish their point of view (or lack thereof) is often part of the initial interview, and special care must be taken in light of their recent trauma. This can present quite a challenge. Investigators are tasked with getting information from the scene as quickly as possible, especially if the suspect is still in the area and poses a threat to others. The investigator must be cognitive of the victim's mental and physical state and determine whether there is any inconsistency in the information provided, all while remaining respectful.

An investigator may not have much control over where the initial interview is held, but it is important to remember that the location where the victim is interviewed may adversely affect his or her statement. While immediate information about a suspect or crime is ideal, unless absolutely necessary, victims should not be interviewed in the back of a patrol car. It might also be advisable to avoid interviews at the scene of the crime. If the victim was brought to an emergency room or trauma center as a direct or indirect result of the crime, investigators may have no choice but to conduct an interview at a hospital, though victims might not be willing to discuss the issue at that time. This leads to a type of witness-initiated contamination, wherein a witness to a crime (in this case, the victim) is not cooperating with the investigation. Witnesses may be too traumatized to cooperate; they may also fear retribution from the suspect, be concerned about the repercussions of being somewhere they did not belong, or may simply be embarrassed about the whole incident.

Non-Contaminated Interviews

The following considerations will help avoid contamination during interviews with witnesses, suspects and victims:

- Be cognitive of the environment in which the interview takes place. Although conducting interviews at the police station may be more convenient for the investigator, it could cause stress to the interviewee, who may feel he or she is being treated as a suspect. Interviews of victims and witnesses should occur in an environment where the victim feels safe, comfortable, and away from distractions associated with the investigation.

- Interviews should be conducted by one interrogator. An individual is more likely to provide information if he/she feels the information is being shared with only one other person. Most people do not feel comfortable providing information to an audience. Having one investigator present allows the interviewee to concentrate on what that investigator is saying. Multiple interviewers often lead to multiple questions. This can have negative repercussions on the lead investigator's ability to build rapport with the victim or witness, increases the likelihood that someone would ask contaminating questions, and often impacts the flow of information.

- Questions should facilitate a narrative response from the victim or witness. Asking "closed-ended" questions results in single word responses. If the investigator doesn't ask the right questions, the interviewee will not provide all of the information they have. Asking open-ended questions will require the interviewee to give a narrative response.

- Focus on the non-verbal behavior of the interviewee. Does the person look agitated, angry, sad, or remorseful? Identifying the non-verbal behavior will often help the investigator determine how to approach the interview. The interviewer should also be cognitive of all non-verbal behavior. If the investigator says one thing, but his or her body language gives a different meaning, effective communication will be disrupted.

- Avoid repeating questions. When questions are repeated, the interviewee may conclude that the answer he or she provided was unacceptable and change the answer. This is particularly true when the interviewee is a child.

- Separate witnesses. Witnesses who are allowed to interact will often compare observations and may change any observations that don't "match up." Additionally, if witnesses share information, they may end up with cumulative recall, telling the investigator that they saw more than they really did.

- Be respectful of witnesses and victims. Depending on the trauma associated with the event, there may be inconsistent statements, hesitation to talk, or hostility from interviewees. If the investigator reacts negatively to these situations, it may greatly influence the communication, and therefore the amount of information, provided.

Examples of Closed-ended and Open-ended Questions:

Closed-ended:

- What is your name?

- Are you hurt?

- Where is the suspect now?

- When did this happen?

Open-ended:

- Can you tell me what happened?

- Can you tell me what your relationship is with the suspect?

- What were you doing earlier in the evening?

- What did you do after the suspect left?

Example

Investigators responded to the scene of a sexual assault. At the scene, the investigators are told that the victim has been transported to the hospital.

Investigators were also told that the victim described the suspect as being a white male, approximately 6' 1", medium build, without any facial hair.

The investigators interviewed the victim at the hospital and asked her if the suspect was a white male, 6'1", 195 lbs., and no facial hair. The victim responded by saying, "That is correct." This is an example of close-ended questioning by the investigators.

Documenting the Interview

There are two primary schools of thought concerning the documentation of information obtained from victims and witnesses. Some investigators record video and/or audio of all interviews. Other investigators only record video and/or audio of suspect interviews. Even if the interview is recorded, notes should be taken and a report compiled concerning the information. Some police officers ask the witness to write out his or her own statement.

If the interview is videotaped, there are several considerations to keep in mind. When the recording starts, be sure to give the date, time, and location of the interview. State who is present during the interview. Try to avoid turning off the recorder once the interview starts, but if you must stop the recording, state the time and reason for the interruption. When recording starts again, state the time and ask the interviewee if he or she was asked any questions while the recorder was off. This is to help avoid any allegations that only certain information was recorded. At the end of the recording, state the time that the interview was terminated.

The Miranda Warning applies only to "government activities," meaning the Miranda Warning only applies to law enforcement interviews of suspects. The Miranda Warning should not be given to victims and witnesses, since they are neither in custody nor being interrogated.

FIGURE 3.3: *All interviews must be documented properly to protect the integrity of an investigation.*

A suspect in custody and being interviewed must be read his Miranda Rights, and must acknowledge that he is willing to talk to the investigator before any questioning takes place. The reading of the Miranda Rights, along with the suspect's waiver indicating that he is willing to talk, should always be on any recorded interview.

However, it is permissible to ask the suspect such questions as his name, his date of birth, and his residential address without giving a Miranda Warning. While investigators both interview victims and witnesses and interrogate suspects, non-law enforcement investigators do not give the Miranda Warning to suspects.

Notes are used to assist the investigator's recollection. Even if the interview is recorded, notes should be taken, because sometimes batteries run out and equipment fails. In many jurisdictions, officers and investigators are required to keep all notes and turn them over to the District Attorney when the case is filed.

Pros and Cons of Having Witnesses Write Their Own Statements

Pros:

- The statement is in the witness's own words

- The statement can be obtained while the investigator talks to other people

- Can free the witness from the scene more quickly

Cons:

- Have a tendency to be too brief

- Self-written statements do not cover all of the information that the investigator needs

- People often need to be asked specific questions in order to get full responses

- May hurry through the statement so that he or she can leave

Conduct a Neighborhood Canvass or Survey

It is not uncommon for people who have knowledge about a criminal act to be apprehensive about coming forward with information. Conducting a neighborhood canvass, or survey, is a means of finding these witnesses.

The **canvass** may be conducted by investigators and/or uniformed officers. While some law enforcement officers may handle the crime scene, other investigators and/or uniformed officers may conduct the neighborhood canvass. The officers go door-to-door and attempt to find individuals who may have some knowledge about the crime. The information may relate to the actual crime, or may relate to some historical information of the suspects or victims. Although this is not as interesting as working the scene, the canvass can be a vital aspect of the investigation. The officers document information from the canvass and provide the documentation to the lead detective. Investigators use the canvass form to indicate who needs to be contacted. Two major considerations apply to the canvass: if no one is home, the officer/investigator leaves a business card, asking that the resident contact law enforcement. The second consideration is that if a resident is home, the officer/investigator needs to ask about other people that live at that residence.

Example

A homicide occurred in a house located in a cul-de-sac. Officers conducted a neighborhood canvass and contacted the owner of a residence across the street from the cul-de-sac. The owner of the residence told officers that he had not seen or heard anything. The officers asked if there was anyone else in the residence and the owner told the officers that his son was home. The officers talked to the owner's son, who said that he was in his bedroom, which faced the cul-de-sac when he heard what sounded like three gunshots. He looked out the window and saw a male run to a car on the corner of the street and leave. The boy was able to provide the officers with a physical description of the suspect and the vehicle, including the license plates. The suspect was apprehended later that same day.

Document the Scene

It is critical to document the scene of a crime. There are three primary ways of documenting a scene: sketching, video recording, and photographing.

FIGURE 3.4: *The art of documenting a crime scene has been improved and enhanced through technology.*

Sketching a scene provides the responding officer with a good reference of what the scene looked like when the officer arrived. It also provides measurements that are not always found in the videotaping or photographing of the scene. The sketch should always contain the date, location being sketched, and the phrase "Not to Scale." When taking measurements associated with items depicted in the sketch, make sure that the measurements are from fixed objects, thus allowing the measurements to be reconstructed by someone else if needed.

Many departments video-record and photograph major crime scenes. Larger departments equip their patrol officers with video cameras and digital cameras to photograph scenes and injuries. When done correctly, videotaping captures everything in the scene, and allows other investigators who aren't at the scene an opportunity to view it in its entirety. Always turn the sound off while videotaping a scene. All too often, someone says something that shouldn't have been recorded. When recording, always make sure to give the date, time, location, and remember to identify who is holding the camera.

The advent of digital photography has been of great benefit to law enforcement. Using a memory disc rather than using film that has to be developed provides two major advantages. The photographer can readily see whether the photograph was good or not. If the photograph doesn't capture what the photographer intended, it can be deleted and the photographer can take another picture. Another major advantage of the digital camera is that a photographer can take as many pictures as are needed or wanted. There is no excuse for not taking photographs of everything in any given scene.

The major rules concerning photographing a scene are:

- Before taking photographs, place the following information on a placard to be photographed before taking pictures

  - Case number

  - Victim's name

  - Location

  - Date and time

  - Name of person taking photographs

- Photograph evidence before evidence being seized

- Take wide-angle pictures and move in toward the evidence, ending with close-up photographs of individual items

- Have the photographs overlap so that there is a frame of reference between photographs

- Take general view photographs of the scene

  - Front of building, showing the house or business address

  - Landmarks, such as street signs

  - Houses and property adjacent to the scene

  - Overall views of each room

- Take medium view photographs of the scene

    - Spatial relationship between specific items of interest and other items in the room or area

- Take close-up photographs of pieces of evidence and/or objects

    - First photograph should be with a ruler or some other type of measurement device

    - Second photograph without measurement device

Initial Incidence Report and Forms

Along with the Crime Scene Log (see Exhibit A in Resources at the end of this Module) and the Canvass Report (Exhibit B), another critical document associated with the initial investigation is the Initial Incidence Report. This form, sometimes called the "offense report," is critical to any investigation, as it contains the summary of the alleged crime, victim and witness information, suspect information, and what occurred during the initial investigation. Some agencies require all responding officers to write a report of their activity. Their reports are called "supplemental reports," and are tied to the offense report. Other reports that are often associated with the initial investigation of a major crime include:

- Serious Bodily Injury Form

- Medical Waiver

A Consent to Search form (Exhibit C) is used to show that a person "knowingly" and voluntarily gave consent to search an area the person has an interest in, such as his home or car. A doctor signs a Serious Bodily Injury Form to show the victim sustained a serious bodily injury, which in many states is an element of first or second degree assault. The signed Medical Waiver allows investigators to obtain medical treatment records which otherwise would be unavailable to the investigators.

Other Considerations

One of the most difficult aspects of an initial investigation for a new investigator is determining what constitutes evidence. **Locard's Principle** holds that whenever a crime occurs, the suspect both leaves something at, and takes something away from, the scene. At every scene, there is "trace evidence" left behind. The suspect puts his hands on the windowpane, steps in the garden, or scratches the victim; in all these situations, the suspect leaving something behind. The suspect may have hair or cloth fibers that he either left or took from the crime scene. By having a complete picture of what the suspect did while committing the crime, the investigator has a better idea of what may be evidence of the crime. When in doubt, collect the item(s). If it is later determined that the collected item(s) are not evidence associated with the case, it will not be introduced at trial. On the other hand, if potential evidence is not collected and is later found to be evidence associated with the case, the results could be catastrophic.

Effective investigations are a result of teamwork. No one person can fulfill all of the roles associated with an investigation. The neighborhood canvass, maintaining the crime scene, interviewing witnesses, and interviewing the victim often occur simultaneously. Additionally, we don't all look at things the same way, or have the same life experiences. As such, one person may notice the significance of some aspect of the case that others missed. Most importantly, sometimes investigators may get too close to an investigation, and need the input from peers to keep things in perspective.

As stated at the beginning of this section, not all crime scenes require the same steps. For instance, crimes such as theft and burglary may not require setting a perimeter. Some considerations that apply to all crime scenes are preserving evidence, separating witnesses, and compiling good notes.

The preliminary investigation is a multi-task responsibility and requires the full attention of the investigator handling this phase of the investigation. Mistakes made during this phase could result in a failed investigation, or valuable evidence being lost or suppressed by the court.

CASE STUDY

A corporate investigator received a report of a theft of property from one of the company's warehouses. The warehouse supervisor reported that over $50,000 worth of merchandise is missing. There were no signs of forced entry and the security guard did not report any suspicious activity during the night. The warehouse supervisor reported that all of the merchandise was accounted for when an inventory was done a week ago.

How would you conduct the investigation?
What are some of the concerns?
Who would you interview?

Summary

Most investigations are initiated with a 911 call or a citizen's call for assistance. Responding officers have to make sure they respond to the scene as safely and quickly as possible. Once at the scene, officers must make the scene safe, render aid to any injured people, and preserve the crime scene. In preserving the crime scene, officers establish inner and outer perimeters. Only law enforcement personnel working the scene, the coroner's office, and medical personnel are allowed inside the inner perimeter. The outer perimeter is established for the news media, the victim's family, or witnesses that need to be interviewed. Three forms are associated with the initial investigation: the initial report, the crime scene log, and the canvass report. All three are critical documents for various reasons, and all will be referenced throughout the investigation.

In the initial phase, investigators are concerned with two types of contamination: contamination of any evidence; and contamination of information received from witnesses and victims. There are several actions that investigators need to take to ensure the crime scene is not contaminated. There are also several actions that investigators need to take to ensure witness/victim information is not contaminated.

Three forms are associated with the initial investigation: the initial report, the crime scene log, and the canvass report. All three are critical documents for various reasons, and all will be referenced throughout the investigation.

A neighborhood canvass is an integral part of any investigation. The canvass helps identify people who have information concerning the case, but had not come forward on their own.

Determining what qualifies as evidence is often a difficult proposition. What is evidence in one case is not necessarily evidence in another case. Any evidence that is collected must be properly bagged, logged in, and secured.

Locard's Principle holds that whenever a crime occurs, the suspect leaves something at the scene and takes something away. This is a premise that all investigators should keep in mind when conducting an investigation. Good investigators are constantly asking what has been left at the scene and what has been taken away.

Effective investigations are a result of teamwork. One person acting alone cannot effectively handle all of the aspects associated with an initial investigation.

Discussion Questions

1. How do you know if something is evidence or not? Are witnesses' observations or physical evidence more reliable? Give examples.

2. A victim tells you that she was getting ready for bed when an unknown male entered her bedroom and sexually assaulted her. How would you avoid contamination of information?

3. What do you feel are the most challenging aspects associated with an initial investigation? Explain.

4. What effect do incomplete or erroneous notes have on a criminal investigation? During the investigation? At trial?

Exercises

1. While driving east on a highway, an intoxicated driver decides to drive down the middle of two eastbound lanes. The driver's car collided with two cars that were well within their lanes. One of the vehicles veers across the westbound lanes, collides with a fence and ends up in a golf course pond. The second car that was collided with veers to the right and rolls down an embankment. What would be the inner perimeter of this case? What concerns does this scene present?

2. A suspect confessed to killing his girlfriend and placing her in a chest of drawers. The suspect said he put the chest of drawers in his truck, drove into the mountains, and dropped the chest of drawers down a steep embankment. Investigators found the chest of drawers, lying approximately twenty feet down an embankment off a mountain road. What are the

potential crime scenes? What would be the inner perimeter? What are some concerns associated with this scenario?

3. A suspect enters a convenience store. He goes up to the counter and asks the clerk for a pack of cigarettes. When the clerk turns around to get the cigarettes, the suspect shoots her. The suspect jumps the counter, takes the cash out of the cash drawer, grabs some cigarettes, and leave through the front door. A customer who comes into the store approximately ten minutes after the robbery finds the victim. What would be the inner perimeter? What are some concerns associated with this scenario?

4. Assume you are responding to the scene of an armed robbery. You are asked to interview the victim to the crime. Discuss the pros and cons of the following ways to take the statement:

   a. Have the victim write out his own statement
   b. Interview the victim and write/type up the statement yourself
   c. Audio record the statement
   d. Video-tape the statement

5. Obtaining uncontaminated information from witnesses is a critical aspect of any investigation. Provide four ways of helping to ensure that the information you receive from the witness is uncontaminated.

Resources

The Exhibits on the following pages are sample forms that are typically used during criminal investigations.

- Exhibit A: Crime Scene Log

- Exhibit B: Canvass Report

- Exhibit C: Consent to Search

Exhibit A

SAMPLE FORM
CRIME SCENE LOG
EXHIBIT A

Initial Officer Preserving the Scene: _____

Case Number: _____   Date: _____

Location: _____

Officer's Name: _____   Badge Number: _____

Time In: _____   Time Out: _____

Activity at Scene: _____

_____

_____

_____

_____

_____

_____

_____

_____

_____

_____

_____

_____

_____

_____

Exhibit B

SAMPLE FORM
CANVASS REPORT
EXHIBIT B

Date: _____   Time: _____
Location: _____
Was anyone home?   Yes ☐   No ☐
If not, was a business card left at the residence?   Yes ☐   No ☐
If someone was home:
Name: _____   Date of Birth: _____
Address: _____
Work Phone: _____   Home Phone: _____
Cell Phone: _____   Email Address: _____
What the person saw or heard: _____
_____
_____
_____
_____
_____
_____

Date: _____   Time: _____
Location: _____
Was anyone home?   Yes ☐   No ☐
If not, was a business card left at the residence?   Yes ☐   No ☐
If someone was home:
Name: _____   Date of Birth: _____
Address: _____
Work Phone: _____   Home Phone: _____
Cell Phone: _____   Email Address: _____
What the person saw or heard: _____
_____
_____
_____
_____
_____

Exhibit C (1 of 2)

SAMPLE FORM
CONSENT TO SEARCH
EXHIBIT C

Middleton Police Department

I, _____ do hereby make the following voluntary statement:

1. I have been informed that I have the constitutional right to require police officers to obtain A search warrant before any search is made.

2. I have also been informed that I have the right to refuse to consent to any search without a warrant, and that no search will be made without a warrant unless I give my consent.

3. No threats or promises of any kind have been made for the purpose of obtaining my consent to search. I do not expect to receive any payment, reward, or other compensation for giving consent to search.

4. Having been informed of the aforesaid, I HEREBY GIVE MY CONSENT TO A SEARCH and I hereby authorize any police officer acting on the behalf of the State of Colorado, in the County of _____, to conduct a complete search of the following property: _____ ,said property being located at _____ , in the City of _____ , and the County of _____ .

5. I also hereby consent and agree that such officer(s), are authorized by me to seize and take possession of any property found in said search, which is stolen, or which is designed, or intended for use as a means of committing a criminal offense, or which is or had been used as a means of committing a criminal offense, or of which is illegal, or which would be material evidence in a subsequent criminal prosecution.

Exhibit C (2 of 2)

SAMPLE FORM
CONSENT TO SEARCH
EXHIBIT C

Person Authorizing Search: _____

Date: _____ Time: _____

Witness: _____ Witness: _____

_____

Items Seized and Removed:

_____

_____

_____

_____

_____

_____

_____

_____

_____

_____

_____

_____

The above items were removed with my permission. I acknowledge receipt of a copy of this documentation.

Date: _____ Time: _____

Officer/Investigator: _____ Badge Number: _____

Signature: _____ Case Number: _____

Key Terms

Chain of Evidence: the documentation of when evidence was received, who handled it, and who processed it. A proper chain of evidence establishes that the evidence has not been altered or compromised.

Canvass: an attempt to contact people in the area of the crime.

Closed-Ended Questions: questions that only require a "yes" or "no" response.

Contamination: any activity related to an investigation that compromises the information being received.

- **Investigator-initiated contamination:** When an investigator, either intentionally or unintentionally, provides a witness with misinformation.

- **Witness-initiated contamination:** When a witness, either intentionally or unintentionally, provides an investigator with misinformation.

Inner Perimeter: the area of a crime scene that should only be accessed by personnel working the case.

Initial Response: the officers or investigators that are the first to arrive at a crime scene; also known as the preliminary response.

Locard's Principle: the principle that is the foundation of trace evidence; sets forth the premise that something is always left and taken from a crime scene.

Make the Scene Safe: ensuring that there is no danger present at the crime scene.

Outer Perimeter: the area of a crime scene where people other than those working the scene such as the medic may congregate.

Preserving the Scene: the process of protecting evidence relating to a crime.

Traditional Interview: questioning that is characterized by "who, what, when, where, and how" questions.

MODULE 4
Advanced Investigations

Key Module Concepts:

- Sources of information available to investigators when conducting the follow-up investigation

- The importance of NCIC and state databases in conducting investigations

- Definitions of link analysis and chronologies and examples of where these tools would be utilized

- The impact of ethics and situational ethics on an investigation

- The differences between civil and criminal liability

Introduction

Sometimes an investigator may obtain enough information during the course of the initial investigation to make an arrest or close out an investigation. More frequently, after the scene and all evidence have been secured and initial interviews conducted, the investigation moves into the second phase, called the follow-up investigation. Seldom is there a clear line distinguishing where the initial investigation ends and the follow-up investigation begins. During this phase, an investigator may use a number of resources to assist in the investigation. This Module will discuss some of the more common resources available to investigators.

Any discussion about resources must address what standards are required to obtain the requested information. Some of the resources discussed in this Module are only available to law enforcement. Other resources are available to anyone who is willing to pay a fee to obtain the information, and some are available to the general public at no cost.

When requesting personal records, such as bank or telephone records, law enforcement must comply with the Fourth Amendment of the U. S. Constitution, which protects citizens from unreasonable searches and seizures. Law enforcement complies with this standard by one of three methods:

- Obtaining consent for the person who has an interest in the records

- Obtaining a search warrant for the information

- Obtaining a subpoena

The Fourth Amendment and its requirements will be addressed in a subsequent chapter.

Non-law enforcement investigators, who cannot obtain search warrants, are not bound by the rules laid out in the Fourth Amendment. Evidence seized by private investigators may be admissible in court, though it might be rendered inadmissible in court had a law enforcement investigator obtained the same information without consent, a warrant, or a subpoena.

Ask Yourself

- *What sources are available to investigators during the follow-up investigation?*
- *What type of liability is an investigator exposed to during the course of the case?*
- *How can the use of a chronology and link analysis assist an investigator?*

Investigative Tools

Criminal Histories

The **National Crime Information Center (NCIC)** is a computerized index of criminal justice-related information which contains such information as criminal histories, arrest warrant information, stolen property, and missing person information (see Figure 4.3). This national database is only available to federal, state, and local law enforcement agencies, and is operational 24 hours a day, every day. The database is accessible via a licensed computer or the law enforcement agency's dispatch. The information within the database is provided by the FBI and federal law enforcement agencies, as well as by state and local agencies.

Additionally, each state has a crime information center that contains a database similar to NCIC, but limited to that state's information. As with NCIC, only authorized law enforcement officers can access the database. Most states have a provision by which a private citizen can pay a fee and obtain a criminal history. Private citizens, private investigators, and corporations all may utilize this service. Personnel with access to both NCIC and state databases may opt to use the state site, as it may take longer to access information from NCIC.

Example

A police officer pulls over a vehicle for a traffic violation. By using either a licensed computer program in the police vehicle or calling dispatch, the officer runs the vehicle license plates through NCIC and/or the state database. NCIC will show whether the vehicle and/or license plates were reported stolen from anywhere in the United States. Running the state database will furnish the same information, providing the vehicle had been stolen in the state.

When the officer obtains a driver's license number, he or she can run the information through NCIC and the state database and find out if the driver has a restricted, suspended or revoked license. The officer can also find out whether the driver has any outstanding arrest warrants, or whether the driver is on probation or parole.

FIGURE 4.1: *Officers have various databases at their disposal when background information on an individual is needed.*

Investigators will use NCIC to perform a nationwide search of an individual's history. The resulting printout will show all arrests anywhere in the United States, along with a brief description of the underlying charges and any time served in correctional facilities.

Was the individual arrested for similar crimes? Who is his probation or parole officer? What is the individual's last known address and who are the individual's known associates? These are a few of the items that the investigator will be able to access.

As with any other database system, the system is only as good as the information entered. If an investigator fails to enter the VIN of a suspect vehicle, known associates of a crime, or other information pertinent to the case, valuable evidence may be lost.

Background Checks

Background check is a generic term relating to the process of obtaining information concerning an individual. The background check may include criminal history, any licenses the individual has held, civil judgments, property, and financial records. Background checks can be compiled by law enforcement agencies, privately owned companies or private investigators. Not everyone has access to the same background databases. Some web-based companies purchase individuals' data and sell it online. Some private companies or private investigators pay a high premium to be able to access certain databases. The fees associated with the background checks vary with the database being utilized. Some background checks do not require the use of a database; instead checking with various institutions, such as schools, banks, county clerk's offices, courts, and the Department of Motor Vehicles, provides necessary information.

The following information can be obtained via a background check:

- Employment history

- Business affiliations

- Military records and discharge status

- Social security number records

- Insurance policy information

- Property ownership

- Residential history

- School records

- Medical records

- Driver's License records

- Immigration status

- Sex Offender Registry status

- Criminal and civil litigation history

- Credit rating

Keep in mind that not all of this information is readily available to all investigators. Law enforcement investigators must obtain consent, a search warrant or a subpoena to get any information that is not publicly available. Failure to comply with this requirement may result in the evidence being suppressed at trial. The investigator may also face civil liability if the information was illegally obtained.

Business Records

Access to and review of **business records** is important for
investigators working fraud cases. These cases can include credit
card fraud, consumer and business fraud, securities fraud, identity
fraud, and computer fraud. Business records cover a wide range
of documents, such as employee lists, memoranda, employment
contracts, bank records, contracts, invoices, and accounting
records. Retention periods for business records are established
by legal requirements and internal policies, and may vary from
state to state and even from company to company. Businesses
that are regulated and/or licensed by the state are required to
maintain records and make them accessible to governmental
regulatory agencies. Secretary of State Offices contain records
of limited liability companies (LLC), limited partnerships, trade
names, trademarks, company officers, registered agents, and
real estate investment trusts. Investigators can also learn if the
company is currently "active" or "inactive." Investigators should
obtain information about companies that are classified as inactive,
because records may contain information pertaining to the company
address, their registered agent, board of directors, and mission
statement that is still relevant and up-to-date.

These and other records maintained by a company in the regular
course of business are admissible in court under the Federal Rules
of Evidence, even though they contain hearsay information. The
reason such information is a hearsay exception lies in the court's
recognized premise that information kept "in the regular course of
business" is assumed to be true. Therefore, the actual records can
be introduced into evidence without having a person testify as to the
original source of the information.

Bank Records

In order to search **bank records**, law enforcement investigators
need either consent of the account holder or a search warrant,
while non-law enforcement investigators need either consent of an
account holder or a subpoena. Such records provide information as

to account holder name(s), signature cards, balance history, bank deposits and withdrawals, wire transfers, and most importantly, transfers to other accounts. Such information is important when investigating cases involving theft, insurance fraud, securities fraud, embezzlement, and even homicide. In civil investigations, bank records may be relevant to divorce, custody, or bankruptcy proceedings. Subpoenas and warrants are usually served upon a corporate officer or the registered agent of the bank. If the records are sought after a case is filed, or during the course of a grand jury investigation, a subpoena duces tecum may be served on the custodian of the records. A *subpoena duces tecum* means that the person being served the subpoena must bring the requested records with them to court. Investigators should also be aware that banks are required to notify account holders if a search warrant has been executed on an account.

Medical Records

Medical records are documentation of a person's medical history and care. In most cases, the medical records are stored at the facility where the patient received treatment, but they may also be filed at the medical provider's off-site administrative offices. Medial records contain information such as, but not limited to:

- Family history

- History of major illnesses or traumas

- Medications the patient takes or has taken

- Surgical history

- Immunization history

- X-rays, charts and test results

Release of medical records is governed by the **Health Insurance Portability and Accountability Act (HIPAA)**, which in part protects patient confidentiality, and any state requirements that govern such information. The rules governing the destruction of medical records may also differ from state to state.

The patient and the care provider are the only people who have an automatic right to review a patient's medical records. Other people wishing to review a patient's medical records must comply with HIPAA regulations. An investigator wanting to review medical records of an individual must either obtain written consent from the patient, or obtain a court order (search warrant). In very specific situations, a criminal investigator may obtain some patient-related information without obtaining a consent waiver from the patient. Most jurisdictions recognize such exceptions as child abuse and/or the sexual assault of a child.

Physicians may also provide investigators with medical information that is not treatment related. For example, when a patient is being treated for an injury, the physician can tell the investigator how the patient was injured, whether the injury is classified as a "serious bodily injury," or whether the victim was sexually assaulted. The physician can also provide the criminal investigator with a recovered bullet, clothing or other potential evidence.

It is recommended that investigators review HIPAA guidelines regarding the release of medical records. Some medical facilities charge for copies of medical records. Insurance companies, civil attorneys, and private investigators often utilize such databases.

The Medical Information Bureau (MIB) is an information clearinghouse founded by insurance companies to help them reduce insurance fraud. Approximately 15 million Americans and Canadians are on this database, and approximately 600 insurance firms use the services of the MIB to obtain information about applicants for life insurance and individual health insurance policy applicants. MIB is a consumer-reporting agency that is subject to the federal Fair Credit Reporting Act and is not subject to HIPAA regulations. This information may be obtained via a subpoena or search warrant. Often, only the relevant parts of a patient's medical record are subject to review. The relevance of the information is frequently determined by the judge conducting an in camera (also called "in chambers") review of the documents, and determining what records will be available to the litigating parties.

The **National Insurance Crime Bureau (NICB)**, which investigates insurance fraud, has access to medical records as a result of the insured waiving the privacy privilege. Some people argue that patient confidentiality is sacrificed in exchange for insurance coverage, because a representative of the insurance carrier is reviewing the medical history. This allows insurance investigators and corporate investigators another avenue to obtain medical records.

In addition to providing medical treatment information, medical records may also provide information concerning health care providers, insurance carriers, and next of kin. This information can lead to additional information concerning claim history, address history, and other facts that may be relevant to the investigation.

Credit Card Records

As is the case with many personal records, law enforcement must either obtain consent or a search warrant to review credit card information. The records can provide information concerning account holders, card activation date, transaction activities, payments and residences. Such information is critical in investigations involving theft, embezzlement, robbery, and homicide.

Telephone Records

Both law enforcement and non-law enforcement investigators use phone records, particularly cell phone records, to help locate individuals. **Telephone records** are part of personal data that is routinely bought and sold online. Some online companies will provide outgoing call information from a previous billing cycle for a fee. Some private investigators also provide a similar service. The information they provide may include the date, times, and duration of the calls during the last billing cycle. This information is more difficult to obtain for incoming calls and call locations.

Law enforcement agencies obtain cell phone information via search warrants or consent. Telephone record information includes customer name and address, rosters of outgoing and incoming calls, duration of call, and the associated telephone numbers. Often investigators are also able to obtain "cell tower" information, which gives a general location of where the calls originated.

The Internet has databases that provide such information such as the name, address, and cell phone carrier of the subscriber. Some of these online sites require a fee for additional information. A commonly used service is the reverse directory, which provides the name associated with a given cell phone number. Private investigators, who can defray the cost to the client, utilize such databases, while law enforcement agencies primarily use search warrants.

Investigators working homicide or missing person cases use phone records to ascertain with whom the person last spoke or when the last call was made. A subscriber can get a detailed list of every phone call that was made during the last billing period, including to whom the call was made and the length of time of the call. If an investigator obtains consent of the subscriber, the information is usually obtained more quickly than if the investigator had to get a search warrant. If a person is missing or is a suspected victim of kidnapping, the phone company can be called and the investigator can obtain phone records and cell tower information. Investigators can also "ping" a cell phone to see exactly where the phone is located. This is especially critical to law enforcement investigators who are attempting to locate a missing person or a suspect. If the investigator is conducting a civil

FIGURE 4.2: *Telephone records are useful in many different types of cases.*

investigation, a subpoena may be used to obtain these records.

School Records

School records encompass information such as report cards, enrollment information, incidents, discipline, medical records, attendance, and emergency notification. Education records are protected by a number of federal and state statutes and regulations. The Federal Education Records and Privacy Act provides that schools or educational institutions receiving federal funds for education may not release school records without the consent of the student or legal guardian. There are both criminal and civil penalties for violating this act. There is an exception for law enforcement when accessing the information for "law enforcement purposes," but keep in mind that other state laws or regulations may supersede this exception. A school may release records if an emergency situation arises that threatens the health or safety of a student or other individual. This would include such situations as kidnapping and missing persons.

Some databases allow educators and parents to access student information including scheduling, attendance and discipline records, test results and transcripts. Law enforcement investigators who are not sure if the records are publicly accessible should err on the side of caution and obtain a warrant or consent.

Some school information may be obtained by contacting a School Resource Officer; this position is held by a uniformed patrol officer who is assigned to an individual school or to a group of schools. By being available in the school on a routine basis, the students often become comfortable with the School Resource Officer and may provide information on who is dealing drugs, bullying other students or dabbling in other undesirable behavior. They may also have some insight into who associates with whom. The Resource Officer also may know about the academic and social problems students are having at school, or even what some students have to deal with at home. Some schools have their own private security officers, who may also be a great source of information.

Public Information Records

Public information records provide a wealth of information that is available to both law enforcement and non-law enforcement investigators. obtaining this information does not require a search warrant. Public records include vital statistics records, bankruptcy filings and business holdings. See Figure 4.3 for a more complete listing.

Information Listed in NCIC (Available to Law Enforcement Only)	Confidential Information consent, warrant (law enforcement) or subpoena (non-law enforcement) required for access	Public Information: All Information Available to the General Public, For Free or For a Fee
Wanted Persons List	Medical records (including immunization history and test results)	Vital statistics (birth, death and marriage records)
Missing Persons List	School records	Adoption records (limited)
Terrorists	Credit history	Business holdings
Juveniles who have committed a delinquent act who have fled their jurisdiction	Bank records	Aircraft title information
Individuals who have committed a felony in a foreign country that has an extradition treaty with the U.S.	Telephone records	Bankruptcy filings
Known threats to the President of the United States		Trademarks filings
Violent gangs and known members/affiliates		Department of Motor Vehicle Records (limited)
Stolen vehicles (including boats)		Liens
Stolen guns		Military records
Orders of protection		Property records
		Inmate locators
		Sex offender registries

FIGURE 4.3: *A listing of the information available to different types of investigators.*

Link Analysis and Chronologies

In addition to the various sources of information discussed previously, there are a number of tools that can be invaluable to an investigator during the course of the investigation, and later at trial. Two tools that are useful in documenting and presenting a case are link analysis and chronologies.

Link Analysis

Link analysis is a means of exposing associations among individuals, enterprises, or activity. Linking information includes telephone numbers called, financial transactions and familial relationships. The link analysis chart may be as simple as a drawing showing the association, or as sophisticated as a computer generated program specifically designed to show links between associates.

During an investigation that involves multiple players or multiple transactions, the investigator should start with a rough draft of the link analysis. As the investigation evolves, the link analysis provides a visual representation of what the case has established. The link analysis also provides insight into what is lacking in the investigation. By the completion of the investigation, the various associations are graphically illustrated.

Link analyses assist the investigator in explaining the case to other investigators, supervisors, clients, or the District Attorney. A link analysis is also beneficial when identifying crime patterns and validating criminal intelligence data. Prosecutors often use link analyses during trials to show the jury the association between the defendant's activity and the activity of another person. This tool is very helpful in racketeering, drug, or gang cases.

The Basic Premise of Link Analysis

Businesses/enterprises are represented by squares, while circles represent individuals. Solid lines between squares and/or circles represent a known association that can be supported by testimony or physical evidence. A broken line between squares and/or circles represents a suspected association that is not supported by testimony or physical evidence. Circles inside of squares represent an individual who is a principal or member of the organization. Using these basic aspects of link analysis, the investigator can illustrate known associations and see where additional investigative work is necessary.

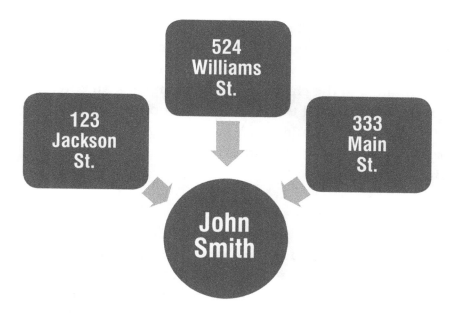

FIGURE 4.4: *Example of a link analysis.*

In this simple link analysis, it shows that three properties are associated with John Smith. The solid arrows denote that the investigation established a relationship between Mr. Smith and the three properties. If the investigation established a relationship among the properties, an arrow would be drawn between the two properties that were established to have a relationship.

A broken line or arrow denotes that there may be a relationship between Mr. Smith and the properties, but the investigation has not established the relationship.

Chronologies

A **chronology** is a means of arranging events according to when they occurred. The main investigative purpose of a chronology is to clarify the chain of events that the investigation has established. It is an evolving document, changing as new information is learned. It illustrates what time periods are accounted for and what time periods need additional investigation. Most investigators also insert the source of the information for each entry on the chronology. This helps the investigator when drafting the arrest warrant, and assists the prosecutor in determining which witness can testify to the information contained in the chronology. For example, if an entry shows that the suspect visited the victim's residence at 10:30 p.m. on August 10, 2010, there would also be an entry that the source of that information was a neighbor who knows the suspect and saw him enter the victim's residence.

This tool is helpful in most types of investigations. Many homicide investigators start a chronology as soon as they are assigned a case. Child abuse cases, especially those involving severe head injuries, use a chronology to help doctors establish when the injury occurred. This is a tool that has great applications for any investigator. Like a link analysis, the chronology can simply be a list of times, dates, and activities, or it can be a sophisticated computer-generated document.

Example of a Chronology:

January 3, 2010 (7:00 p.m.)	Sam Ellison went to Warren Schaeffer's house and told Mr. Schaefer that Mr. Ellison needed Mr. Schaeffer's help in "taking care of a little problem." (Warren Schaeffer's interview with law enforcement investigators on 01/06/2010)
January 3, 2010 (8:00 p.m.)	Mr. Schaeffer met Tom Collins at the Wal-Mart, located at 1234 Main St. per Mr. Ellison's instructions. Mr. Schaeffer and Mr. Collins purchased a five-pound dumbbell and some duct tape. (Warren Schaeffer's interview with law enforcement investigators on 01/06/ 2010)
January 3, 2010 (8:45 p.m.)	Mr. Schaeffer and Mr. Collins met Mr. Ellison at the corner of 1st Street and Wadsworth Avenue. Mr. Ellison got in Mr. Schaeffer's car and told Mr. Schaeffer where to drive. (Warren Schaeffer's interview with law enforcement investigators on 01/06/2010)

| January 3, 2010 (9:10 p.m.) | Mr. Ellison called the victim and told her that he would be at her apartment at 10:00 p.m. (Warren Schaeffer's interview with law enforcement investigators on 01/06/2010 and Mr. Ellison's cellular phone records.) |

Investigative Issues and Systems

How Non-Law Enforcement Can Bridge the Gap in Interagency Relations

Law enforcement has historically been a "closed" institution. The nature of the work and stresses associated with the job unite law enforcement officers. When an officer requires assistance, officers believe that the only source that can be relied upon consistently is another officer. They believe that no one else can truly understand what it means to be a police officer, and they take care of one another. If you are a police officer in one organization, you are recognized and accepted in other law enforcement agencies. If you are not a police officer, you may not have access to "insider information."

There are multiple examples of major criminal investigations in which one law enforcement agency doesn't share information with another. Law enforcement themed television shows and movies often portray local/state law enforcement agencies' distrust and lack of communication with federal law enforcement agencies, most notably the FBI. Local agencies do not want their cases taken by another agency. Sometimes agencies are concerned about being upstaged by another agency.

In today's mobile and highly technological society, the need to effectively interact with multiple agencies to combat multi-jurisdictional criminals is critical. Criminals readily move among various jurisdictions, committing crimes in multiple cities and counties. If investigators fail to communicate across jurisdictions, valuable information could be lost. Another reality is that the more cases that are established against a particular suspect, the greater the chance of a conviction or a plea agreement, because a defendant might agree to in order to serve less time than they would be sentenced to in a jury trial in exchange for a guilty plea.

Bridging the gap between agencies may be a challenge. It is the responsibility of the individual investigators handling the cases to go beyond any political competition or issues between departments and put together the best case possible. Everyone associated with the investigations should keep in mind that the ultimate goal is to convict people who commit crimes and keep innocent individuals from being wrongly charged.

Non-law enforcement investigators face unique challenges. Investigators who have previous law enforcement experience often have strong contacts. If the non-law enforcement investigator is working on civil cases, the law enforcement investigator may be more inclined to provide information. Law enforcement investigators are more hesitant to help non-law enforcement investigators working criminal cases.

Non-law enforcement investigators who don't have previous experience as law enforcement investigators, or who left law enforcement with a tarnished reputation, often face an uphill struggle in getting cooperation from law enforcement agents, who may see criminal investigations in black and white terms. Law enforcement investigators may not see their non-law enforcement investigator counterparts as true investigators. The bond that ties law enforcement officers together re-enforces the separation from those who do not share the same experiences.

How can this gap be bridged?   If a non-law enforcement investigator demonstrates good investigative skills, can communicate effectively, and conveys the attitude that he/she is also working to find the truth rather than to get a client off at all costs, there is a better chance of effective communication. It is not an easy task, and may only develop over time. One of the worst things a non-law enforcement investigator can do when attempting to communicate with law enforcement investigators is to demand access to information, or to be openly critical of how the law enforcement investigator handled the case.

Non-law enforcement investigators have an advantage over their law enforcement counterparts in several respects. Non-law enforcement investigators do not have the authority to arrest; thus, people may be more inclined to talk to them. Law enforcement investigators may portray the attitude that people must cooperate, while the non-law enforcement investigator has to sell the idea of cooperation. Potential witnesses associated with the defendant are more likely to talk to a non-law enforcement investigator. Additionally, the non-law enforcement investigator is not restricted by the policies and procedures of a law enforcement agency. He/she is also not restricted by the paramilitary structure of a law enforcement agency. Law enforcement investigators all too often rely upon their position to elicit information, while the non-law enforcement investigator must rely upon personality and communication skills.

Ethics

Ethics is a system of moral values that govern conduct. Moral values come from statutory law, customs, policies, and community standards. Some organizations have written codes of ethics that govern conduct. Others may have an unwritten code of ethics pertaining to their job. Ethics is also a means of evaluating conduct. Law enforcement investigators may perceive private investigators as not having any ethics, and vice versa. Law enforcement investigators may be perceived as doing anything to get a conviction, while private investigators may be perceived as willing to do anything for a quick payday. A written code of ethics that everyone within the agency is expected to adhere to helps ensure that everyone is acting in the best interests of the investigator.

Law enforcement investigators have departmental policies and procedures to address ethical considerations, and a written code of ethics to which all members of the department must adhere. Many non-law enforcement investigators do not have a written code of ethics. Their perception of what constitutes ethics is more subjective.

Any discussion concerning ethics must address the concept of **situational ethics**. According to the situational ethics model, any given situation dictates what decision is made, rather than the decision being based on fixed laws or customs. As this concept relates to investigations, decisions should be made based upon what is just, rather than on the "letter of the law." Examples of situational ethics are found all around us. In certain situations, we may condone lying, cheating, assault, and even homicide. Acceptance of the concept of situational ethics impacts any code of ethics. Although situational ethics are dealt within law enforcement agencies, it may not be to the degree the concept is found in the private sector, primarily due to set code of ethics policies and procedures found in law enforcement agencies.

Codes of Ethics

Each law enforcement agency has a Code of Ethics by which officers must conduct themselves. To read the Code of Ethics from the Riverside County (CA) Sheriff's Office, go to:

http://www.riversidesheriff.org/department/ethics.asp

(R)

While not required, reputable private investigators agencies will often have a Code of Ethics. Investigators who are self-employed but who are affiliated with professional organizations will adhere to that organization's Code of Ethics, as well. To see the Code of Ethics for the California Association of Licensed Investigators, go to:

http://www.cali-pi.org/?Ethics

FIGURE 4.5: *Law enforcement officers must be careful not to overstep into excessive or illegal use of force.*

Use of Force/Color of Authority

Use of force and color of authority are concepts that apply to law enforcement only.

Use of force is the use of physical restraint by a law enforcement officer when dealing with a citizen, including holding, choking, striking, and/or the use of pepper spray, Taser, baton, or a firearm. Law enforcement officers are empowered to use the appropriate amount of force to make arrests, and to protect themselves and members of society. Any time an officer or investigator uses force to make an arrest or protect themselves or others, the amount of force the officer uses will be scrutinized. For example, if an officer is making an arrest and the suspect pulls away from the officer, the officer can use appropriate force to affect the arrest. If the suspect is merely pulling away and is not threatening the officer or anyone else, the officer would not be justified in pulling his gun. This would be considered **excessive use of force**. Appropriate force in that situation may be striking the suspect or using a Taser, while pulling a gun and threatening the suspect would be considered excessive force.

Illegal use of force refers to situations where a police officer uses force in violation of a law or statute; for instance, a police officer using lethal force on a person who merely takes a fighter's stance and raises his fists would be considered illegal use of force.

Both excessive use of force and illegal use of force have civil and criminal ramifications. Police departments have written policies concerning the use of force. Violations of these policies could result in disciplinary action against the officer ranging from a disciplinary letter in his/her personnel file, unpaid time off, or termination. The biggest factor in determining if the officer used excessive force is a review of the amount of force the officer used in relation to the degree of resistance from the suspect.

Color of authority (or color of law) is associated with law enforcement's use of authority. Such authority includes power to detain, arrest, search, file charges, and even use deadly force in certain situations. Abuse of that authority could result in an officer being disciplined, terminated or even criminal charges filed.

Legal Liability

Legal **liability** indicates that a person is financially and legally responsible for his actions, or in some instances, his failure to act. Legal liability may have both civil and/or criminal implications. When a law enforcement investigator arrests an individual, the arrest must be based upon probable cause. If the investigator meets that standard, and conducted the investigation in an honest, ethical manner, there is no liability exposure. If the investigator created evidence or excluded evidence that would help establish the defendant's innocence, liability exists. The difference between civil and criminal liability is that civil liability can result in fines or dismissal from the job, while criminal liability can result in incarceration. Criminal liability requires "intent," but as it relates to law enforcement, some negligent acts could result in criminal liability. If a patrol officer is responding to a dispatch call and uses his red lights and siren, he is still responsible for the safe operation of his vehicle. If that officer enters an intersection and causes an accident, he may be both civilly and criminally liable for any injuries that are a result of the accident.

Liability can attach to both the individual and the agency. If a police officer shoots and kills a person and the investigation establishes that the officer was not adequately trained in the appropriate use of a firearm, the individual officer and agency can be sued. For any criminal liability claim to prevail, it must be shown that the officer had intent.

Law enforcement agencies carry civil liability insurance. The individual investigator may be covered under the agency policy, but if the investigator is being sued, it may be in the investigator's best interest to retain his or her own attorney. If an individual sues a law enforcement agency and the policy adjuster determines it would be best to compensate the complaining party rather than take a chance on paying a higher amount as a result of a trial, the individual investigator or officer may be upset with that decision. It may appear to the officer that the insurance company is conceding that the officer did something wrong, though in some instances, it is merely a matter of economics.

For examples of police liability, please see Figure 4.6.

Police Liability Term	Definition
Excessive Force	Use of more force than is necessary to affect an arrest. If a suspect was just being non-compliant, use of a baton or firearm would be considered excessive force.
Failure to Perform a Required Duty	Covers multiple situations, such as failing to prevent or intervene when the officer witnesses a person committing a crime
False Arrest	Making an arrest without probable cause
False Imprisonment	Unlawful or illegal detention of a person for any length of time
Malicious Prosecution	A civil action alleging that prosecutors intentionally and maliciously used their position to file criminal charges against someone. The most common allegation is that the criminal filing lacked probable cause, which leads back to the initial investigation and arrest.
Perjury	Lying under oath
Pursuit of Offenders	Commonly used to refer to high-speed pursuits. Officers must weigh the type of offender being pursued against the risk that high-speed pursuits present to the general public.
Unlawful Force	Force that is not justified under the law. As it relates to police officers, an example would be shooting through the passenger window of a car when the driver or passenger will not open the door.
Unlawful Stops/Searches	Officers allegedly create a reason for stopping a person when neither reasonable suspicion nor probably cause exist. An example would be stopping a driver for running through a stop sign when he/she in fact came to a complete stop.

FIGURE 4.6: *Examples of Police Liability*

Summary

During a follow-up investigation, investigators have time to conduct more in-depth interviews, obtain search warrants, and use resources that may not be available during the initial investigation.

One of those resources is the National Crime Information Center (NCIC) database. This database is a tool that allows law enforcement to access a wide-range of information concerning suspects, stolen vehicles, missing persons, and outstanding warrants. Each state has a similar database that covers state related information.

Background checks are another investigative tool that provides access to information concerning victims, witnesses, and suspects. Some of the information is publicly accessible, meaning law enforcement does not need to obtain a search warrant. Other background information requires law enforcement to obtain either consent or a search warrant, such as (but not limited to) bank records, school records and medical records.

There are a number of investigative tools that assist all investigators. Two that were discussed in this chapter were link analysis and chronologies. Both tools can be instrumental to conducting investigations, but also serve well during trials.

Law enforcement agencies don't always communicate well with one another, and the communication between local law enforcement agencies and federal agencies can be strained. Individuals who are not part of the law enforcement community may face difficulty in getting local law enforcement to work with them. Private investigators have a better chance of having effective communication with law enforcement if they have a law enforcement background, or if law enforcement agents see the private investigator pursuing the truth, rather than criticizing the law enforcement investigation or doing what they can to get their client off.

Finally, law enforcement ethics are codified, while many private or corporate investigator ethics are implied. If a law enforcement officer violates the department's code of ethics, the officer may be disciplined or even fired. Private or non-law enforcement investigators do not necessarily face the same consequences.

Discussion Questions

1. Discuss the various situations in which a police officer or investigator may need to use force. Determine what degree of force would be acceptable and what degree of force would be unacceptable.

2. You are an investigator assigned to conduct an investigation of the following scenario:

    A woman filed a complaint alleging that she has received threatening phone calls from her ex-husband, who moved out of state two months ago. In his threats, the ex-husband said he will take their two children from her, move out of state, and she will never see them again. The woman also said that a day before he left the state, the ex-husband beat her and their 15 year old son. The woman decided not to file charges on the assault because her ex-husband was leaving the state.

    • What are the potential crimes?
    • Should there be an investigation even if the victim doesn't want to pursue the case?
    • How would you investigate this case?

3. You are an investigator assigned to conduct an investigation of the following scenario:

    A person alleged that he gave $50,000 to a man named Warren Schaeffer and that Mr. Schaeffer was to invest the money on behalf of the victim. Mr. Schaeffer said the victim should expect a return on his investment within two months. It has now been five months and the victim has not received any money. The victim has repeatedly called Mr. Schaeffer's telephone, but it always goes straight to his voice mail.

- What are the potential crimes?
- How would you establish that this is a crime rather than a poor business venture?
- Is there any special investigative assistance that may be needed in handling this case?

4. Your assignment is to gather information about a suspect who may be a serial murderer wanted in three states. What resources would you use, and what information would you expect to get from those resources?

Exercises

1. Chronologies are a helpful tool in establishing an overview of what occurred during a crime. Using the Internet or some other source, find an example of a crime and draft a chronology of what happened.

2. Draft a link analysis of the association of various members of your family. The link analysis should contain the association of people, addresses, and telephone numbers.

3. In this chapter we discussed the various sources of information that is available to investigators in conducting a background check. List the various types of information that would be available about you. Example: Your birth certificate would provide the name of your parents, as well as when you were born. You should be able to list at least ten sources of information.

4. Describe the difference between "excessive use of force" and "unlawful use of force." Using the Internet, find four examples of "excessive use of force," as well as four examples of "unlawful use of force."

5. Find three different examples of a "Code of Ethics" pertaining to law enforcement and private investigations. Compare and contrast the various codes of ethics you found.

Key Terms

Background Check: a database and interview check of an individual's history, including employment, criminal activity, and places of residence.

Bank Records: any records maintained by a banking institution; includes account holder information, deposits, and withdrawals.

Business Records: any records pertaining to the composition and activity of a company.

Chronology: an investigative tool used to visually represent activities of a case in reference to one another; it is also used to show when what activity was done during the course of an investigation.

Color of Authority/Color of Law: acting under the appearance of the law; a criteria used to determine if an officer's action was authorized under the law.

Consent: an exception to the warrant situation; for a person's consent to search to be admissible, the consent must be given "knowingly" and not as a result of any threat or intimidation.

Criminal Histories: a listing of an individual's arrests and convictions.

Ethics: a system of principles; may be either moral or established by a group.

Excessive Force: using a greater degree of force than is needed to either control the situation or make an arrest.

Felony: the criminal punishment the has a minimum sentence of one year in the Department of Corrections.

HIPAA: Health Insurance Portability and Accountability Act; protects the confidentiality of a patient's medical records.

Illegal Use of Force: refers to situations where a police officer uses force in violation of a law or statute.

Interagency Relationship: the interaction among the various law enforcement agencies; i.e. local, state, and federal.

Liability: financial responsibility for an individual's actions.

Link Analysis: an investigative tool used to show the association between people, places and/or things.

Medical Records: includes dates and locations of medical treatment, attending physician, treating hospital, ambulance service, type of treatment, and medical history.

NCIC: National Crime Information Center. A national database that contains criminal histories of individuals, fugitive information, missing person information, and other criminal justice related information.

NCIB: National Insurance Crime Bureau. An agency that has an insurance industry database containing claim information, as well as investigators who help insurance agencies and local law enforcement in the investigation of insurance fraud.

Public Information Records: records that are open to the public and do not require a warrant or consent; examples include bankruptcy records, deeds, civil actions, and trademark information.

School Records: contains emergency contact information, information concerning the student's performance, disciplinary actions at school, and family information.

Situational Ethics: a term to describe how ethics may change depending on a given situation.

Telephone Records: statements that contain subscriber and service information, incoming and outgoing call rosters.

Use of Force: use of physical restraint when controlling an individual.

MODULE 5
Crime Scenes

Key Module Concepts:

- The various components of a sketch

- The various types of sketches associated with an investigation

- Three basic types of measurements used in compiling a sketch

- Know the concepts associated with crime scene photography and digital recording

- Differences between direct and circumstantial evidence

- General principles associated with the collection of evidence

Introduction

After the scene has been made safe, investigators can turn their attention to processing the scene. What happens during this phase will be a major factor in determining the success of the investigation. Failure to document the scene properly, or failure to preserve evidence, could result in an unsolved case, in a guilty person being acquitted, or in an innocent person being charged. A number of tools are available to investigators to help ensure the scene is documented. Use of these tools both assists in conducting a professional investigation and in presenting the case during a trial. These tools are available to law enforcement and non-law enforcement investigators alike.

Ask Yourself

- *What are the various means of documenting a crime scene?*
- *How do you take effective pictures of the crime scene?*
- *How should you collect evidence?*

Sketching

Two levels of communication occur when someone tries to describe an area, a building, or a room: a person provides the description, while another person receives (sees or hears) the description. If the receiver does not have the same frame of reference as the speaker, the description may be incomplete or inaccurate. Even if the description is very detailed, it may fall short of providing a complete mental picture of the location. If the description explains where various items are located in the building or room, the mental picture is even harder to recreate and relate. If a "picture" is created to help describe the area, the speaker has a better chance of effectively communicating specific information. Sketching, which is the creation of a crime scene illustration, is one means of providing a picture for various audiences involved in an investigation.

Advances in technology provide investigators with instantaneous pictures of a crime scene. Digital cameras, camcorders, and cell phones allow investigators to not only capture images immediately, but to readily share those images with other investigators, witnesses, or the D.A. Because of these advances, some police officers and investigators don't place the same importance upon sketches as in previous years. However, sketching is still a valuable tool for the investigator for a number of reasons.

Sometimes a camera or camcorder may not be available or may malfunction. More importantly, images on a camera or camcorder are one-dimensional and are not always able to capture the overall view of the scene, such as the interior of the entire residence where the crime occurred. A sketch, also referred to as a diagram, can easily show dimensions of a room and the distance between various items/evidence found at the scene. A sketch can represent what may be difficult to put into words. Lastly, a sketch provides an effective means of recall for the investigator or officer who drafted it, as there may be months between when the drawing of a sketch and a trial.

Sketches come in several forms. The officer or investigator who responds to the crime scene compiles a rough sketch. It may be nothing more than the investigator drawing an overall view of the scene in a notebook or on draft paper. Another type of sketch may be used by prosecutors to show a jury the crime scene and the location of evidence. This type of sketch helps witnesses supplement their testimony by showing where the witness was when the crime occurred, the location of pieces of evidence, or what the scene looked like. This type of sketch, which is usually drawn to scale, is more sophisticated than the rough draft. At the most sophisticated level, sketches can be computer generated, 3-D, and/or contain animation. This type of sketch is often used in vehicular homicide, assault cases, as well as in large civil suits.

A sketch may be admitted into evidence as long as it meets the admissibility standards of relevance and accuracy. Use of sketches is not limited to law enforcement investigators and prosecutors. Defense attorneys, civil attorneys, and non-law enforcement investigators use sketches as investigative or explanatory aids. Just as investigators don't photograph or video-record all crime scenes, sketches are not applicable to every crime scene. Sketching is appropriate at all violent crime scenes, such as homicide, sexual assault, and vehicular assault/homicide. Sketches may provide both an overview and close-up of the scene or of specific pieces of evidence.

Types of Sketches

There are two basic types of sketches: a rough sketch and the finished or scale sketch. The **rough sketch** is the first pencil-drawn sketch of the crime scene and the location of the objects and evidence therein. Since this sketch is most often done at the scene, it is usually not to scale. It is not uncommon to have one of the investigators on scene be responsible for the rough sketch. Only one investigator should be assigned to draft the rough sketch. The sketch should be done after the scene has been photographed, but prior to moving any evidence.

The advantage of a rough sketch is that it affords a ready reference and a mental picture for investigators who are not on the scene, but will be involved in the follow-up investigation. It also is a refresher aid used to prepare for courtroom testimony.

The **finished sketch** is the sketch that may be used for formal presentation of the case or for trial. When used for trial purposes, the finished sketch can be used to assist witnesses in their testimony. It is especially helpful for witnesses to show movement throughout the scene or location of various people and/or things.

A number of crime scene sketching programs are available to investigators, including:

> The Cad Zone: a computer program designed to generate site plans, and crime scene diagrams

> Sirchie: a company that provides a number of investigation related products including crime scene sketching tools

> Smart Draw: a visual processor built exclusively for Windows 7, Vista, and XO

> 3D Eyewitness: a crime and accident scene reconstruction software

> AutoCad: a computer aided design software program for two-dimensional and three dimensional designs

Drafting a Sketch

Rough sketches should be done in pencil. If the investigator uses a pen, any mistakes would require either crossing out incorrect information or starting the sketch over. When the sketch is not drawn to scale, the phrase "Not to Scale" should be put on the sketch. The whole piece of paper should be used when setting the boundaries of the sketch. All too often, an investigator makes the boundaries too short and there is not sufficient room in the sketch to place all of the items. If a large number of items are to be shown, it may be more effective to use a numbering system and describe the items in the legend, which lists the details of, and the items depicted in, the sketch.

Example of a Legend:

Legend:

- Item #1: Handgun

- Item #2: Victim's Body

- Item #3: Victim's Purse

The legend should also contain the following information, which is universally required in sketches:

- Investigator's name

- Case number

- Type of investigation

- Date of sketch

- A north arrow (used in diagrams to indicate which direction is north)

- The words "Not to Scale" (if the sketch is not to scale)

One of the most important components of any sketch is measurement. Depending on the crime, relevant measurements may include dimensions of the room and location of, and distance between, different pieces of evidence at the crime scene. It is vital to both obtain accurate measurements and to measure in such a fashion so that others can reconstruct your measurements at a later time. Whenever possible, use a steel tape measure for obtaining measurements; as the tape itself not stretch, it provides a more accurate measurement. Use conventional units of measurement such as inches and feet. If an investigator's **point of origin**, or starting point within a sketch, is not a fixed object, others will not be able to reconstruct the measurements accurately. Therefore, all measurements should be from fixed locations, such as walls, trees, telephone poles, curbs, or immovable objects.

Example

The point of origin is a chair in the room where the crime occurred. If the chair were moved, any reconstruction of the measurements from the chair would be inaccurate.

Investigators use three methods to accurately obtain measurements of items located within a scene:

Rectangular Method: This method requires that the investigator measure out from a wall until he is at a ninety-degree (90°) angle from an object, then measures from the ninety-degree (90°) point to the object

Baseline Method: From a fixed point, the investigator runs a baseline, and then takes measurements at right angles

Triangular Method: This method is not often used. It uses a permanent fixed point as a starting point, such as a corner of a room, telephone pole, or fire hydrant. Then in a straight line, the investigator measures out to a point perpendicular to the object being measured, and then from that point to the object.

Examples of Crime Scene Sketch Methods

Rectangular Method:

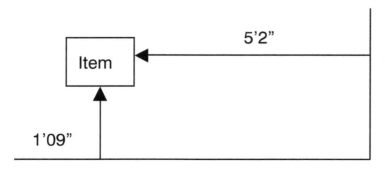

Baseline Method:

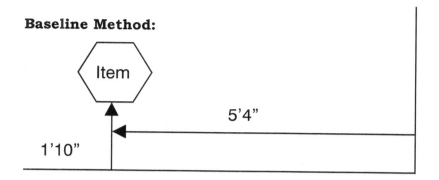

Triangular Method:

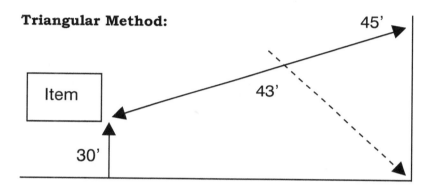

The materials needed to make a sketch are readily available and easy to store. Paper, pencil, a steel measuring tape, ruler, eraser, and a strong writing surface will readily suffice.

Investigative Photography

When associated with crime scene investigation, photography and video recording can be divided into two categories: crime scene photography and follow-up investigation photography. Although these categories share many of the same characteristics, there are some important distinctions.

Crime scene photography is one of the most important tools used to document a scene. The number one purpose of crime scene photography is to capture the crime scene in its original, unaltered state. Toward that end, photographs and/or video recording should be completed prior to any evidence collection or any disturbance of the scene.

Keep in mind the two primary goals associated with crime scene photography:

- Documenting the scene as it was found

- Ensuring that the photographs are admissible in court

Two types of photographs are necessary to crime scene investigation. Wide-angle pictures provide an overview of the area and a frame of reference to items in the scene. Most wide-angle photographs start with a picture of the exterior of the house, the block on which the house is located, or a nearby intersection. In some cases, an aerial photograph is very helpful. In cases that involve numerous criminal acts, or when the crime scene is in a rural area, aerial photographs provide a frame of reference no other photographs can provide. Such pictures show the proximity of the various crime scenes to each other and to where the defendant lived or worked. After photographs of the overall scene are taken, the photographer should take some "mid-range" photographs, and proceed to the close-up photographs.

Close-up images show details of evidence. For instance, an investigation of an assault in the living room of a private residence is underway. Wide-angle photographs would include photographs of the exterior of the house and photographs of the living room from the entrance of the house. Close-up photographs would be detailed images of the broken vase on the floor in the living room, the phone cord disconnected from the wall, and the bloodstains on the carpet.

Investigators must be systematic in the taking of photographs. It does not matter if you photograph the room in a clockwise or counter-clockwise fashion. What matters is that the entire area is covered. Once the crime scene is photographed and processed, an investigator can never re-construct the scene to cover what was missed during the photography phase of the investigation.

There can never be too many pictures of a crime scene. This is especially true with the advent of digital cameras. Investigators can take a picture and examine it thoroughly before taking the next photograph. If the photo does not capture what the investigator wanted, or if there is something wrong with the image, the investigator can delete the photograph and take another. Armed with a digital camera, a memory card, and a good flash, there is no excuse for a lack of photographs that capture the scene.

As mentioned earlier, do NOT move items during this phase of the investigation. Remember the primary purpose of crime scene photographs is to capture the scene as it was found. Moving an item to get a better picture is not acceptable.

Keep a log of photographs taken at the scene. The log will help avoid confusion as to what the picture is depicting. The photo log also provides a reference of what pictures were taken, which is helpful when discussing the case with other investigators or when preparing the case for trial.

Another important aspect of crime scene photography that can be overlooked relates to photographing evidence. After the investigators have taken initial pictures of the scene and the investigation is moving to the evidence collection phase, it is recommended that two pictures are taken of items that are collected. The first photograph is of how the item was found. The second photograph is with a ruler or some other measuring device in the photograph.

The benefit of digital photography goes beyond the ability to take a multitude of photographs and immediately evaluate the quality of each photograph. Digital photographs can be enlarged, affording an investigator to see detail in the photograph that is unavailable with 35mm film cameras. A number of computer programs are available to remove backgrounds, enhance the lighting, and make other modifications to digital photographs. Courts will allow such enhancements as long as the content of the photograph is not changed.

While crime scene photography documents what was found at the scene, follow-up photography primarily deals with forensics. Forensic photography produces images that are associated with the forensic investigation of a case, including photographs of bullets, clothing, and fingerprints. **Forensic photography** falls under the category of follow-up photography, but not all follow-up photography is forensic in nature. Wide-angle pictures of pry marks, tire track impressions, autopsy photographs, and fingerprints are examples of forensic photographs.

Although crime scene photography is a very important tool, it is not a substitute for the other tools associated with an investigation. Investigators still need to take notes, draw sketches, and take measurements. Photographs, taken in conjunction with other tools, help investigators to provide an accurate reconstruction of a crime scene.

Video Recording

Video recording is another useful investigative tool that recreates a scene to a degree unattainable with other investigative tools. Video recording provides both an overview of, and insight into the relative relationships among, various aspects of a crime scene.

The same standard governs the admissibility of video recording: is the video a true and accurate representation of the scene? To be as accurate as possible, the person making the video recording should give his/her name, the date, time, and location. Video recording should be conducted in a systematic manner so that nothing is missed. When recording a room, the investigator should start with an overview of the entire room. Once the overview is complete, the investigator should move around the room, recording the floor, walls, and ceilings. The investigator then can focus in on specific pieces of evidence or items of interest.

Two potential problems exist with video recording that do not affect other methods of documenting a scene. If the video image is "jerky," quickly moving from wide-angle to close-up images and for jumping from one location to another, the end result has a negative impact on the person(s) viewing the video. Video recording should be conducted in a smooth, even pace. Focusing on a particular item should also be done with a smooth, slow pace.

The second potential problem concerns audio recording. Once the investigator provides the **introductory information**, or the essential information relevant to the specific recording, the audio function should be turned off. If the audio is on, an investigator may feel the need to narrate the video. Remember, the purpose of video recording is to provide a true and accurate representation of the scene, not for an investigator to provide his opinion concerning the scene. There is also a possibility that other individuals' voices will be picked up, which may result in the video's inadmissability at the trial.

Law enforcement agencies generally use crime scene investigators to record or photograph crime scenes. The lead investigator, or supervisor, is responsible for determining what photographs should be taken. Some departments issue digital cameras to patrol officers to use when conducting investigations that do not require crime lab participation. A partial list of cases where the patrol officer would take photographs includes:

- Domestic violence cases where the victim was not seriously injured

- The point of entry on a burglary case

- Simple assault

- Vandalism

- Automobile accident

Recording Statements

Most agencies advocate the recording of witness and suspect interviews. A major advantage is that recorded statements depict what was said during an interview, dismissing allegations that the investigator misrepresented or omitted information from the case file. It is also a permanent record of the interview. This allows the investigator to make reference to the interview in his report without writing down everything that was said.

Unfortunately, some people may not be as candid if their statement is recorded. Explaining that the interview is recorded to ensure what was said and done during the interview can alleviate this problem. Another potential downside is that a defense attorney may use the recording to attack the investigator's interview method, choice of words, emphasis on various words or emphasis on interview techniques. The more experience an investigator has in recording statements, the better he will be at avoiding areas that may be scrutinized by a defense attorney.

The entire interview should be recorded without interruption. Some investigators conduct a **pre-recorded statement** with suspects, and then record the interview; however, it is recommended that the recording should start when the suspect is first interviewed. Sometimes the person being recorded may ask to go "off the record," meaning that the person wants the recording to stop for a few minutes. The investigator must weigh the benefit of having the interviewee continue interacting with the investigator against the potential for allegations that something happened while off the record, which can impact the admissibility of the statement. If the investigator decides to stop the recording, he should provide a quick summary of what occurred once recording resumes. If an attorney or the parent of a juvenile joins the interview and state they want to talk alone with the interviewee, the investigator must turn off the recorder while he is out of the room.

Any recorded interview should contain the following information at the beginning of the interview:

- The date

- The time

- The location

- Self-identification of each person present for the interview

- An overview of why the interview is occurring

At the end of the interview, the investigator should give the time that the interview was concluded.

Some agencies only record suspect interviews. Other agencies leave recording of non-suspect interviews up to the individual investigator. In situations where the interview is not recorded, it is recommended that the investigator compile the report of the interview as soon as possible and allow the interviewee the opportunity to review the report.

Non-Law Enforcement Investigators

Non-law enforcement investigators do not have the luxury of calling upon a crime scene investigator to take photographs. They have to supply their own equipment and often do not have the same degree of photography training as CSI personnel. The quality of the photograph does not determine whether it will be admitted at trial. If the person who took the photograph can testify that the picture is a true and accurate representation of the scene, it will be admitted into evidence.

Although it is not a universal practice, it is recommended that video recordings be treated as evidence. The original recording disc should be logged into evidence and handled in the same manner as any other piece of evidence. Copies of the original recording can be used for follow-up investigation, ensuring that the original is not damaged or erased. This holds true for audio recordings as well.

Collection and Preservation of Evidence

Law enforcement investigators must have a working knowledge of the elements of the crime under investigation. Evidence is used to establish both the elements and perpetrator of the crime. Without this knowledge, investigators would not know what evidence to collect. In a white-collar crime, evidence may consist of bank records to show that the defendant took possession of the victim's money and spent it on the defendant's own desires, rather than investing it for the victim.

The rule of thumb relating to the collection of evidence is "When in doubt, collect it." During the course of an investigation, hundreds of pieces of evidence may be collected, but by the time of trial, only a small percentage of the collected evidence will be admitted. If the investigator failed to collect evidence that is needed at trial, the chances of going back and obtaining that evidence may be slim or non-existent.

Juries today are more sophisticated than ever concerning their knowledge of the advances in the fields of forensic science. Juries expect expert testimony concerning DNA, bloodstain

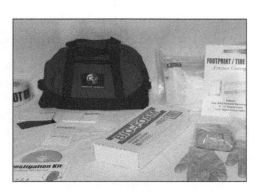

pattern analysis, and latent fingerprints. When they don't receive it, they may conclude that the investigation was incomplete. The result may be an acquittal of the defendant.

FIGURE 5.1: *There are guidelines in place to properly collect and maintain evidence.*

Direct and Circumstantial Evidence

From a legal standpoint, evidence consists of statements and physical items that are presented at trial to determine whether the allegations against the defendant can or cannot be proven. Not all evidence is admissible during a trial. Only evidence that the judge determines to be relevant and reliable will be admitted.

The two basic types of evidence are direct and circumstantial. Direct evidence is testimonial evidence. The testimonies of the victim, lay and expert witnesses to the crime, the investigating officer, and experts are examples of direct evidence. A **lay witness** is anyone who is not an expert, and as such cannot offer an opinion concerning his or her testimony. They may only recount what they personally encountered, without interpreting the experience. **Expert witnesses** are witnesses who are recognized by the court to be more knowledgeable than most people in a specific area.

Psychiatrists, doctors, and DNA analysts are a few examples of expert witnesses. Before the court will allow someone to testify as an expert, the potential witness must testify as to his own expertise. Education, research, published works, and areas of specialization are all considered before the court determines who might testify as an expert. This designation allows the witness to render an opinion.

Not surprisingly, lay witness testimony is not always 100% accurate. Some factors that may impact witness testimony are

- Poor eyesight

- Poor memory

- Being intoxicated or under the influence of drugs at the time of the event

- Anxiety or reluctance over involvement

- Knowing the victim or the suspect

- Fear of retribution

- Fear of being discovered somewhere he/she should not have been (example: teenager who skipped school and went to the movies)

- Involvement in the actual crime

Circumstantial evidence is evidence from which an inference can be drawn. Examples of circumstantial evidence are:

- Blood

- DNA

- Fingerprints

- Hair and fibers

- Impressions and imprints

- Tool marks

- Documents

Circumstantial evidence does not always prove that a crime was committed. If a defendant's DNA profile matches the DNA profile found in a rape victim's rape kit swabs, a jury would reasonably conclude that the defendant had sexual intercourse with the victim. What cannot be concluded from the DNA evidence is whether the intercourse was non-consensual. Likewise, fingerprints found at a scene establish that the suspect was there, but cannot conclusively establish that the suspect committed the crime. The same is true for hair, tire tracks and blood. However, circumstantial evidence taken in conjunction with other evidence may establish that the defendant committed the alleged crime.

It is important to remember that not all evidence is admitted during a trial. The prosecutor or defense attorney may choose not to submit various pieces of evidence. The prosecutor may have five witnesses to the shooting or robbery, but decide to use only three of them during the trial. A defense attorney may have a doctor who is willing to testify that the defendant has a mental condition, but the attorney may elect to argue that the defendant did not commit the crime rather than concede that the defendant committed the crime, but had a diminished mental state.

Other evidence may be suppressed by the court, meaning that the judge has ruled that the evidence will not be admitted. In that case, the jury will not hear the evidence; in a trial to the court, the evidence will not be considered in the judge's decision. The court may suppress evidence from either party (prosecution or defense in a criminal case; plaintiff or defendant in a civil case). **Suppressed evidence** can have a profound impact on a criminal trial where the prosecution has the burden of proving beyond a reasonable doubt that the defendant committed the crime, while the defendant does not have to prove anything. If the only evidence against a defendant is his statement to police, and the court suppresses that statement, the prosecution will not get a conviction. Likewise, if the seizure of the handgun that was determined to be the weapon used in the crime is ruled to be unlawful, the gun cannot be offered as evidence of the crime.

Investigators must ask themselves, "What is evidence?" What qualifies as evidence in one case may not qualify as evidence in another. If the defendant's fingerprints are found in his or her house, the prosecution would not attempt to introduce the fingerprints because it is expected to find fingerprints of a person in his/her own home. However, if the defendant's fingerprints are found in the victim's residence and the defendant denied even knowing the victim, the fingerprints would become important evidence.

Once an investigator determines what the evidence is, the potential evidence must be located, properly seized and preserved. Evidence that is not properly seized and preserved will not be admissible in court. The first consideration for the law enforcement investigator is whether he has a lawful right to seize the evidence (to be covered in a separate module). Assuming the investigator has a right to seize the item(s), the next issue is the proper collection and preservation of the evidence.

Before entering a crime scene or touching anything, the investigator must make sure potential evidence is not contaminated. The investigator wants to avoid placing his prints or DNA on any evidence, and does not want his prints to obliterate any other prints that are on the piece of evidence. This is why investigators must always wear gloves when collecting evidence. With the strides in modern DNA technology, many agencies also advocate that investigators wear a mask while processing a scene, so that DNA from the investigator's mouth and nose does not contaminate potential evidence.

Various tools are used in the identification and collection of evidence. A flashlight, magnifying glass, lasers, and ultraviolet light are used to identify various stains that may contain DNA. Fingerprint powder, fingerprint tape, and latent print cards are needed to lift latent prints. Tweezers, scissors, and a box cutter/ knife are needed to collect hair and fiber evidence. A good camera is needed to take photographs, and casting molds are needed to make casts of shoe prints and vehicle tracks. A measuring tape and ruler are required to show the relative size and dimensions of various pieces of evidence.

Packaging and labeling the evidence is the next critical step. Evidence is packaged to make sure it is not lost or contaminated by other pieces of evidence. A chain of evidence (also known as chain of custody or evidence report), documenting when evidence was received, who handled it, and who processed it, must be created. A proper chain of evidence establishes that the evidence has not been altered, contaminated, or compromised. See Exhibit E, Evidence Report/ Property Tag form in the Resources section, for a sample form.

Certain types of evidence should be packaged in paper bags, while other pieces can be placed in plastic bags or tubes. Heavier items, such as handguns, hammers, and knives, should be secured in boxes. Handguns must be "made safe" prior to being placed into evidence; this means that the gun cannot be fired. Documents should be placed in plastic envelopes. Handling documents in this matter allows investigators to review the content of the document without compromising any latent prints that may be on the document.

Clothing, cloth items, and shoes should be placed in paper bags. Different articles of clothing should be packaged separately and folded as little as possible. If the articles are bloody or wet, the articles should be air dried before being placed in paper bags. Never fold and place wet bloody items in a bag, as the blood will transfer to other parts of the item.

Some items require special packaging, such as charred items, fluids, and items containing hair and fibers. Law enforcement agencies have specific policies and procedures addressing how various items should be packaged. The universal considerations when packing evidence are:

- All weapons will be made safe prior to being placed into evidence

- Bloody items that are wet must be air-dried prior to being placed into evidence

- Evidence containers holding bodily fluids, such as blood, must be clearly labeled as such

- Hazardous liquids must be identified on the evidence bag so that the evidence can be placed in a safe location

- Knives should not be placed in a paper bag

- All items placed in plastic bags are to be heat sealed prior to being turned over to the property bureau

- All pieces of evidence must be properly labeled prior to being turned over to the property bureau. Paper bags will be folded at the top and red evidence tape placed on the bag such that the bag cannot be opened. Tubes will also be secured with red evidence tape.

- No evidence will be accepted without an evidence sheet

Evidence properly submitted to the property bureau is available for any additional testing that may be required. Properly submitted evidence is labeled with a brief description of the item that was seized, the location it was seized from, the case number, the date that the item was seized, and the name of the officer who packaged the item. Any time the property is taken from the property bureau, the person taking custody of the item must sign the property form, listing when they took the item and when it was returned.
When an investigator obtains a sample containing evidence, a **control sample** should also be obtained. For example, if a piece of carpeting is taken because it has a bloodstain, another piece of carpet that does not contain a stain should also be taken.

Additional Information
When an investigator places evidence tape on a container, the investigator must place his initials and date on the tape. Anyone opening the container after it was initially placed in the property bureau must open the container without disturbing the other evidence tape already in place. When the container is re-sealed, that investigator's initials and the date must be placed on the new evidence tape. This shows the chain of custody, meaning the container contains the initials and dates of each person who had custody of the piece of evidence. Original video tapes/discs of interviews and photo lineup photographs should be handled like any

other piece of evidence; they should be properly sealed and placed in the property bureau.

Some items, such as vehicles and furniture, are too large to place in a police property bureau. Vehicles are usually placed in a secure impound lot with evidence tape placed on all the doors and trunk. Furniture and other large items are placed in a secure location off-site, and are subject to the same procedures used for smaller items entered into the property bureau.

Law enforcement investigators who keep evidence in their offices, cars, or homes run the risk of the evidence being ruled inadmissible. Non-law enforcement investigators do not have the same requirements concerning the storage of evidence, but they must show the court that the item was not contaminated or otherwise compromised. Even though private investigators and non-law enforcement investigators may not have access to a "property bureau," they must still demonstrate to the court that the evidence they obtained was not compromised or contaminated.

Summary

Documenting the scene is an important aspect of any investigation. Sketching, photographing, and video recording document the scene for potential courtroom use, but they are also effective investigative aids. Not only do sketches provide an investigator with a means of recall, they provide a visual reference when describing the scene.

Sketches, or diagrams, may be in the form of a rough sketch or more detailed form. There are a variety of computer-based programs that assist the investigator and prosecutor in creating sketches for trial purposes. All sketches should contain certain elements: a north arrow, a legend, the wording "Not to Scale", the officer/investigator's name, the location and the date. One of the most important components of the sketch is to make sure that it accurately represents the scene and that the scene can be reconstructed based upon the sketch.

Photographing and/or digitally recording the scene are excellent ways of documenting the scene. With the advent of digital cameras and memory cards, an infinite number of photographs can be taken of the scene. It is always best to work from the overall scene to the close-ups of particular pieces of evidence. When digitally recording the scene, make sure the sound is off so that there is no danger of the recording capturing something that may result in a suppression at trial.

The accurate recording of the scene is essential. It not only assists the investigators working the case, but also is evidence that helps the jury understand what happened. Recording of witness and suspect interviews is also a good way to ensure the accuracy of what was said during an interview. The skilled investigator becomes very comfortable conducting a recorded interview.

Collection of evidence is a critical part of any investigation. Failure to properly document the collection of evidence, and failure to secure the evidence properly, may result in the evidence being suppressed at trial. Suppressed evidence is of no value to the investigator or the case. Failure to properly document the case and preserve evidence also contributes significantly to ensuring that the guilty are punished and the innocent are not accused.

Discussion Questions

1. What factors could impact direct evidence? How can investigators make sure direct evidence is not compromised?

2. Provide four examples of circumstantial evidence. How do the chosen examples impact a conviction or an acquittal?

3. What are some consequences of improper collection of evidence?

Exercises

1. You are conducting an investigation of the following crime: Two suspects enter a bank, wearing ski masks and bulletproof vests. Both are armed with handguns. One of the suspects shoots a round into the roof of the building and tells everyone to "hit the floor." The other suspect disarms and strikes the security guard, knocking him unconscious. The suspect who fired the shot takes wallets and purses from the six customers. Neither of the suspects is wearing gloves; witnesses describe the suspects putting their hands on the counters and desks in the bank lobby. The suspects leave in a green Chevrolet, which is found abandoned five blocks from the bank.

   a. List the various types of direct evidence available at the scene.
   b. List the various types of circumstantial evidence that is available at the scene.

2. Discuss how you would collect and preserve the following pieces of evidence:

   a. A bloody knife
   b. Hair
   c. A handgun
   d. Fingerprints on a cup

3. Using the example given in Exercise 1, describe how you would go about processing the scene and collecting evidence. Address how you would "document the scene."

4. Assume your classroom is a crime scene. Imagine that a suspect forced open the door and upon entering the room, assaulted one of the occupants. The victim of the assault grabbed a baseball bat and struck the suspect. As a result of being struck, the suspect bleeds on the floor. The suspect grabbed the bat from the victim and strikes the victim. The victim has a bleeding wound and wipes blood on the wall. As the suspect leaves, he drops his wallet on the floor. After your instructor tells you where the items of evidence are located in the classroom, draw a rough sketch of the crime scene. Remember to take measurements of where the items were located.

5. Using a room that you have ready access to, assume you are responding to a crime scene and are assigned to draw a rough sketch of the scene. Use one of the measuring techniques discussed to show where items are in the scene. Remember, a rough sketch is used to provide an overview of the scene. Identify some evidence in your scene and list it in the legend, along with the measurements of where the evidence was found.

Resources

Exhibit D

SAMPLE FORM
EVIDENCE REPORT/PROPERTY TAG
EXHIBIT D

Case Number: _____   Tag Number: _____
☐ Seized Pursuant to Search Warrant   Date: _____

☐ Owner   ☐ Victim   ☐ Finder   ☐ Suspect
Name: _____   Phone: _____
Address: _____
City: _____ State: _____ Zip: _____
Booking Number: _____

☐ Crime   ☐ Misdemeanor   ☐ Felony   ☐ Other
Details: _____

☐ Evidence   ☐ Found Property   ☐ Property for Safekeeping
Description:
1. _____
2. _____
3. _____
4. _____
5. _____
6. _____
7. _____
8. _____
9. _____
10. _____

Recovered By: _____   Serial Number: _____
Date: _____   Time: _____
Location: _____

CHAIN OF CUSTODY

Received From:	By:	Date/Time:
_____	_____	_____
_____	_____	_____
_____	_____	_____
_____	_____	_____

Prepared By: _____   Serial Number: _____
Date/Time Booked: _____   Approved By: _____

Key Terms

Baseline Method: a means of measuring the location of objects or evidence at a crime scene. The investigator runs a baseline and then takes measurements at right angles to the object or piece of evidence.

Control Sample: an uncontaminated piece of material taken from the same area where evidence was obtained. The control sample is compared to the sample with potential evidence to determine similarities and dissimilarities between the two samples.

Crime Scene Photography: refers to photographs taken at the crime scene.

Expert Witness: individuals who are recognized by the court to be more knowledgeable than most people in a specific area; education, research, published works and years of experience are ways of measuring expertise. Psychiatrists, doctors, and DNA analysts a few examples of expert witnesses.

Finished/Scale Sketch: documents for courtroom presentation to assist witnesses in testifying and/or to assist the jury in understanding what the scene looked like.

Follow-up Photography: refers to photographs that are taken subsequent to the crime scene photographs. These are used to assist witnesses in their testimony; may also include forensic photographs.

Forensic Photography: photographs that are associated with the forensic investigation of a case; includes photographs of bullets, clothing, and fingerprints. Forensic photography falls under the category of follow-up photography, but not all follow-up photography is forensic in nature.

Introductory Information: refers to what investigators should always say at the beginning of a recorded interview and includes the date, time, location, and identification of who is present.

Lay Witness: any person who is not an expert, and as such cannot offer an opinion concerning his or her testimony. They may only recount what they personally experienced, without interpreting the experience.

Legend: the part of a sketch that lists the items within the scene, the location of evidence, and other information relevant to the sketch.

North Arrow: used in diagrams to indicate which direction is north.

Point of Origin: a starting point; refers to where an action was initiated. With regard to sketching, it is the object, preferably a fixed object, from which the investigator recreates the scene.

Pre-Recorded Statements: conducting an unrecorded interview of a witness or suspect, then recording the interview after information is obtained.

Rectangular Method: a means of measuring the location of objects or evidence at a crime scene. This method requires the investigator to measure out from a wall or other permanent point to a ninety-degree (90°) angle from the object, and then measuring at a ninety-degree (90°) angle to the object.

Rough Sketch: the first pencil-drawn sketch of the crime scene, and the location of the objects and evidence found there.

Sketching: The act of creating either a non-photographed illustration of a crime scene. The "sketch" may be a rough draft, which is compiled at the scene, or a computer generated sketch used for courtroom presentation.

Suppressed Evidence: evidence that the court has determined will not be admitted at trial.

Triangular Method: a means of measuring the location of objects or evidence at a crime scene. The investigator uses a permanent fixed point as the starting point and measures in a straight line to a point perpendicular to the object being measured, and then from that point to the object.

Video Recording: a method used to document a crime scene. Also refers to the recording of suspect and/or witness interviews.

Notes

MODULE 6
Interviewing

Key Module Concepts:

- The importance of rapport building

- Examples of how to build rapport

- Structured interview techniques

- Ensuring effective communication

- Major types of non-verbal communication

- The most effective means of avoiding contamination of information

Introduction

An interview is one of the most important tools available to an investigator. In basic terms, an interview is a conversation between two or more people; the primary goal of that conversation is to gather information. For an interview to be productive there must be an exchange among the individuals participating in the interview; the interviewer must ask questions that garner specific answers from the interviewee.

Interviewing is a combination of art and science, and the best interviewers refine their techniques over time. Unlike some other tools we discussed, merely learning interviewing principles is not enough to make someone an effective interviewer. Rather, effective interviewers are continually learning various methods; they put those methods into practice by interacting with people. This may be more complicated than it seems. For many individuals, communication doesn't come naturally. Think about someone you know who holds conversations with complete strangers. Those people are often envied, because this is a skill that many people do not possess.

Investigators interact with a wide range of people on a consistent basis. Effective investigators must get detailed, accurate, and truthful information. If the obtained information is incomplete, untruthful, or inaccurate, the investigation can be greatly compromised   There are several principles that apply to all investigative interviews, no matter who the interviewee might be. These principles apply to law enforcement and non-law enforcement investigators alike. Understanding these principles will greatly assist an investigator in conducting effective interviews.

Ask Yourself

How do some investigators always seem to get people talk to them?

- *Is it a question of personality?*
- *Can anyone learn to do this?*
- *What if rapport cannot be established??*

Communication Principles

Communication involves four important parts:

- The sender

- The message

- Channels

- The receiver

The sender formulates a thought, creates the message by putting it into words and sends that message to the receiver. Although the process sounds simplistic, a number of factors can greatly influence the effectiveness of the communication. Some of those factors are:

- The sender doesn't articulate what he/she wants to say

- The communication takes place in a crowded room and the receiver isn't paying full attention to the message

- The message is delivered in words the receiver doesn't understand

- The receiver is "multitasking" when the message is sent, thereby filtering the information

These are just some factors that can greatly impact effective communication. An investigator who is aware of the four parts of communication can help ensure that effective communication occurs.

Although people emphasize verbal communication, at least two-thirds of all communication is non-verbal. An investigator has a distinct advantage if he understands the non-verbal cues presented during an interview. The most common types of non-verbal communication used by investigators are:

Kinesics: interpretation of body language and non-verbal behavior

Proxemics: the study of social distance and spacing

Oculesics: the study of the role of eyes and eye contact in non-verbal communication

Paralanguage: non-verbal aspects of speech, including pitch, volume and tone

Example

John is accused of embezzling funds from the company he works for. During the interview with an investigator, John takes a seat at the furthest end of the table (proxemics). He places his right elbow on the table and sits such that his right side faces the table (kinesics). During the 20-minute interview, John only glances at the interviewer, avoiding any eye contact (oculesics). When asked if he took money from the company, John becomes angry, and starts yelling at the investigator that he is going to sue everyone (paralanguage).

The interviewer responds to John's activities by moving to a chair closer to, and facing, John, and making a conscious effort to establish strong eye contact. In a calm voice, the investigator explains to John why he is being interviewed.

Rapport is the first and most important aspect of communication. Rapport is the process of building a sense of mutual trust, understanding or common ground. Without rapport, little or no communication occurs, and thus little to no information is obtained. Rapport occurs when two people agree on the means and willingness to communicate. Rapport can be result of the interviewer and interviewee sharing some emotion or experience. The connection may be emotional or intellectual. It is important to remember that rapport does not mean that the interviewer and interviewee are always in agreement; it only indicates that there is some degree of understanding between them.

Once rapport has been established, the interviewer can start asking the questions that may shed light on the investigation. While asking questions, the interviewer listens to the interviewee's responses, but also watches the interviewee's non-verbal communication. Maintaining rapport while obtaining truthful, detailed information requires delicacy. The investigator formulates and asks questions, records the answers, and looks for non-verbal cues, all while maintaining rapport with the interviewee.

Additionally, the investigator has to make sure that the information being received is not contaminated. Avoiding contamination of information is a critical aspect of an investigator's interview, for two reasons:

- The contaminated information could be used to impeach the witness in court, thus compromising the witness' testimony

- The contaminated information may result in the investigation going in the wrong direction, wasting time and resources

Investigators must always be aware that they can also contaminate information. If an investigator asks questions that contain or imply an answer to that question, the person being interviewed may assume that what the investigator said is true, even if it was not what the interviewee recalls.

The best way to avoid contamination is to ask open-ended questions and have the interviewee provide a narrative response to general questions. An example of an open-ended question is, "What did you do last night?" This question requires the interviewee to give a narrative response. By contrast, close-ended questions require a "yes" or "no" answer or short response. An example of a close-ended question is, "Were you with Johnny last night?"

Another important aspect of communication is feedback, which is information that the interviewee gives to the interviewer to acknowledge that the information has been received. Feedback may provide the interviewer with additional information and effective interaction with the interviewee.

Feedback applies to both the interviewer and the interviewee, as each must confirm that they have heard what the other has said. The interviewer must also demonstrate to the interviewee that information has been received. One of the most effective means of feedback available to an investigator is reflective listening (previously discussed in Module One). This technique is important to the investigation for several reasons:

- It shows the interviewee that the interviewer is not only listening, but understands the information being presented

- It verifies that there is no misunderstanding as to what the interviewee is saying

- It provides an opportunity to clarify any ambiguous or vague information.

Misunderstood information can negatively impact the investigation; if the investigator mischaracterizes the information, it could be used to impeach the interviewee at trial.

Feedback	Reflective Listening
Communication where a listener provides a response to a speaker to confirm that he or she has processed their message	A type of feedback that involves responding with part of the previous message to make sure information received is clear and accurate
Interviewer: I know this has been very traumatic for you. You are safe now. Before we talk about what happened, do you have any questions for me? Interviewee: Yes. I am very scared and don't know what to do. What happens next? Will I have to testify? What is to prevent him from coming back?	Interviewee: "We got together and drove to the victim's house." Interviewer: "So, if I understand you correctly, you and someone else drove to the victim's house. Who are we? Whose car was used to drive to the victim's house?"
The interviewee confirms that he/she has heard the message and responds appropriately	The interviewer's follow up questions repeats the part of the interviewee's message for clarity and comprehension

FIGURE 6.1: *The differences between general feedback and reflective listening.*

Interview Types

There are two basic types of interview techniques that an investigator will use: traditional and structured.

As covered in Module Three, traditional interviews are usually associated with initial responses to a crime, where the investigators need to get information quickly in order to determine what occurred. The "who," "what," "when, "where," why," and "how" questions are the type of questions asked to provide a quick overview of any situation. Traditional interviews do not rely on rapport building to the same degree that structured interviews do. Frequently, a patrol officer or investigator will respond to a scene and have little idea of what occurred. Traditional interview questions are asked in quick order, with the assumption that the interviewee will answer them. Time is usually of the essence, especially if the suspect might be in the area or the victim is missing.

A **structured interview,** which is usually used during the follow-up investigation is markedly different from the traditional interview. A structured interview requires organization, the building of rapport and the use of open-ended questions to ensure that specific information is gained.

Structured interviews are often portrayed on television when a detective is interviewing a victim, witness, or suspect at a police station. This type of interview occurs when the investigator has more time to think about his/her approach, more time to conduct the interview, and more time to formulate questions. Some of the important aspects of a structured interview are:

- **The ability to pick the time and location of the interview.** Rather than responding to a scene, the investigator can determine the best time and location to conduct the interview. Sometimes it is better to conduct the interview at the police station, while other times it is more effective to conduct the interview at the individual's residence. Timing of the interview may also be important. Is it better to conduct the interview in the morning, afternoon, or evening? The investigator has more control of these aspects in a structured interview than he does during a traditional interview.

- **The ability to prepare for the interview.** In the structured interview, the investigator has time to prepare for in-depth questioning. Criminal history, ties to other individuals associated with the crime, and additional information concerning the crime can help the investigator to maximize the results of the interview. Knowledge of the case and individuals associated with the case helps the investigator determine if the interviewee is being deceptive, and why the deception is occurring. Knowledge also provides investigators with insight as to how to increase the probability that the individual will provide information.

- **Rapport building is a critical aspect of a structured interview.** Unlike television portrayals, not everyone is willing to talk to investigators. Investigators must be able to establish a dialogue, in which questions are asked and the interviewee provides information. If rapport is not established, information will not be obtained. This applies to all potential interviewees who may not wish to be questioned. Victims may not want to cooperate for fear of reprisal from the suspect, because of involvement in the crime, or a lack of desire to get the suspect in trouble. Witnesses may not want to get involved for a variety of reasons, while suspects may distrust investigators.

FIGURE 6.2: *Building rapport is an important investigative skill.*

CASE STUDY

A woman makes a 911 call and tells the dispatcher that she had just shot her estranged husband, who had entered her house and threatened to kill her. When investigators arrived at the woman's apartment, they found a deceased male lying in the doorway of the apartment with a gunshot wound to the back of his head. A spent bullet casing was found in a box fifteen feet from the front door.

The investigators take the woman to the police station for an interview. As an investigative interviewer, what types of questions would you ask? Is there any information you would want to obtain prior to conducting the interview?

Interviewing Victims, Witnesses, and Suspects

While all interviews incorporate the fundamentals we discussed earlier in this section, interviewing victims, witnesses, and suspects each have their own unique characteristics. How these interviews are handled impact the investigation and the potential trial. There are a couple of principles that apply to all interviews. For instance, do not allow witnesses to interact with each other or with the victim. This could lead to contamination of evidence. Attempt to make witnesses and victims comfortable, maintaining a professional demeanor. Don't provide witness and victims with any information concerning the case.

Victim Interviews

Prior to the actual interview, the investigator should evaluate the mental and physical status of the victim. Asking the victim if they need anyone or anything conveys a sense of caring and concern. It also provides the investigator with a benchmark of how the victim is feeling. Avoid the question "How are you feeling?" Such a question may be perceived as patronizing, and may impact the rapport between victim and investigator. If the victim needs medical attention, those needs should be addressed immediately.

At the start of the interview, the investigator must obtain the victim's date of birth, work and home address, contact telephone numbers, a contact person, and educational background. At some point during the interview, the investigator should ascertain if the victim has any physical ailments or issues, including hearing and eyesight problems. These may become issues by the time of trial, especially if there is an issue regarding the victim's identification of the suspect.

Depending on the case, the investigator may need the victim to sign several forms. The most common forms would be a medical release form, if the case involves any physical assault against the victim, as well as a consent to search form (see Module Three for a sample Consent to Search form).

Making the Victim Feel Safe

There are two major categories of considerations when conducting victim interviews. The first deals with the emotional aspects and the second deals with environmental aspects. If the investigator doesn't address the emotional aspects of the victim, there is a strong possibility that the victim will provide incomplete, if any, information.

Emotional Aspects include:

- Making the victim feel safe

- Making the victim feel comfortable

- Providing support for the victim

- Being aware of the victim's needs

The Needs of the Victim may be impacted by a number of factors:

- The nature of the crime

- The age of the victim

- The emotional and mental development of the victim

- The victim's support system

Investigators take all of these factors into consideration when conducting the victim's interview. The nature of the crime plays a major role in helping make the victim feel safe. If the victim was sexually assaulted, the victim may have fear that the suspect will return. If the alleged sexual assault was by a family member, the victim may either fear retribution from the alleged suspect or fear that the suspect will be arrested. In these cases, the victim must be assured that the investigator will do everything within his power to make the victim safe. Depending on the age of the victim, this may include having the victim stay with someone, providing police protection, or involving social services. Victims should be engaged in a conversational manner, and should be informed about the situation at a level that does not compromise the investigation.

Making the victim feel safe is a primary issue in **crimes against persons**, which are crimes that involve direct physical harm or force toward another person. This category of crime includes, but is not limited to, sexual assault and battery, attempted homicide, and domestic violence. It also applies to some **crimes against property**, or crimes that involve the theft, unauthorized use, or destruction of another person's possession. A burglary is a very personal violation, and the victim may feel vulnerable after such an occurrence. Likewise, an auto theft can leave the victim feeling vulnerable because the suspect knows the victim's address (from the vehicle's registration), and may have access to the residence (if he or she has the key ring). It is important for the investigator to address these safety issues before attempting to interview the victim. If the victim doesn't feel safe, there is a chance the victim won't be totally candid about what they know.

Another important aspect of making the victim feel safe is by letting them notify family or other people that can provide a support system. The investigator must explain the importance of talking to the victim alone so as to lessen the degree of information contamination, but also let the victim know that his/her support system is available. The potential problem is that the victim may rush through information with the investigator in order to be with his or her support system.

Make the Victim Feel Comfortable

Making the victim comfortable can create problems for the investigator. Victims often associate police interview rooms with interrogation of suspects; understandably so, since many interview rooms are actually designed toward that purpose. They are not comfortable or welcoming locations. Most of them also contain clearly visible video recording equipment. Victims may feel like they are suspects in such an environment.

The investigator can rectify this situation in several ways. Most importantly, the investigator can make the victim comfortable by explaining that he or she isn't a suspect. If the victim is not a suspect, do not read them the Miranda Warning. A victim who is advised of their Miranda Rights is very likely to stop talking. The investigator can also offer the witness something to drink or eat, and explain where the restrooms are. If possible, the investigator should give the victim an idea of how long the interview will take. This allows the victim to have a degree of control, as lack of control leads to discomfort.

Law enforcement investigators should consider removing their guns and badges while conducting interviews; if they keep these items on, the items should be covered with a coat. Additionally, an investigator who appears to be comfortable in the interview setting makes the victim feel comfortable as well.

FIGURE 6.3: *Making the victim feel comfortable can create a smoother interview process.*

Non-law enforcement investigators have an advantage in this area, as their environment is usually more user friendly. There is no interrogation room stereotype, and victims don't have the impression that they are going to be arrested.

Other Considerations

As mentioned in Module Three, the victim should not be allowed to talk to any other potential witness at the scene, as this could lead to contamination of information. Ask the victim if she spoke to anyone else. Ask the content of the conversation, and the name and contact information of the person.

An ongoing issue in various law enforcement agencies is whether or not to digitally record a victim's statement. The prevailing procedure is to digitally record all interviews, if possible. There is no statutory requirement concerning the recording of statements. Investigators should inform the victim that the interview is being recorded. Many departments request that victims write out their own statements, because the statement is in the victim's own words and is not in response to specific questions. This can be advantageous in that sometimes victims only answer the investigator's questions and don't offer information. Having victims write their own statement may result in additional information. However, some victims write very little. If the victim writes his or her own statement, the investigator should read the statement and ask any follow-up questions the investigator may have prior to the end of the interview.

Contrary to what is seen on television, victims may be interviewed a number of times. As the investigation progresses, new information is compiled that may require the investigators to contact the victim. It is important that at the conclusion of each interview, the investigator lets the victim know that there may be additional interviews.

In some cases, a victim becomes a suspect. Because of this, investigators should be careful not to provide too much information to the victim, which could compromise the investigation. An investigator must always interact with victims with a guarded empathy.

CASE STUDY

Police respond to the scene of a one-car collision. Inside the car is a nude female whose hands are tied. After providing the female with clothes, the woman tells investigators that earlier in the day, she stopped at an unknown intersection and an unknown man got into her car. The assailant forced the victim to change seats. The assailant drove the victim around for several hours, during which time he sexually assaulted her. While on the floorboard of the front seat, the victim pushed on the brakes and grabbed the steering wheel, causing the vehicle to crash into a tree. When the car crashed, the assailant ran away. The victim told investigators that she had both long-term and short-term memory loss from an automobile accident three years ago. Because of that, she doesn't remember if the assailant had sexual intercourse with her.

During the course of the investigation, investigators learn that the victim is married and had spent the day of the alleged incident in a bar with two men, drinking and playing pool. Two witnesses saw the victim in a car outside the bar, kissing one of the men she had been playing pool with.

What are some of the issues concerning this case? How would you approach these issues with the victim?

Witness Interviews

A witness is someone who has information concerning a crime. Witnesses may be neighbors of the victim, friends of the suspect and/or victim, relatives, business associates, or acquaintances, or people who witnessed the crime. Witnesses may end up being suspects in the crime or codefendants of the suspect. The information a witness supplies may have been acquired "firsthand," meaning it is something the witness saw, heard, or participated in. The information may also be circumstantial, meaning it is information that isn't firsthand, but has something to do with the crime.

Firsthand Information	Circumstantial Evidence
An armed suspect pulls into a gas station and gets out of his vehicle. A witness, who is putting gas in his own vehicle, watches the suspect go up to the cashier window, pull a gun, and shoot the cashier.	Later that evening, the suspect goes to his uncle's residence and is upset. The suspect tells his uncle that he was mad because he had just killed a cashier for six rolls of pennies.

As covered in Module Five, there are two basic types of witnesses: lay witnesses and expert witnesses. Lay witnesses include citizens, police officers, and victims. They can testify about anything the witness obtained through their five senses. It is important that investigators not only ask witnesses what they saw, but also what they heard, smelled, or felt. Lay witnesses cannot testify as to their opinion. Expert witnesses are individuals who the court has determined have expertise beyond that of an average person, via their experience and education.

As is the case with victims, no two witnesses are the same. Some may be helpful, some will want to avoid dealing with investigators, and others may have ulterior motives for talking to investigators. Effective investigators have the ability to establish rapport with a wide range of witnesses.

It is very important to ensure that information from all witnesses is detailed and accurately recorded. As with victim interviews, there is no requirement to record witness interviews. Investigators who write up witness interviews should have the witness review the report prior to the investigator turning it in. It is better to correct any errors or misstatements prior to filing the charges and giving the reports to defense counsel.

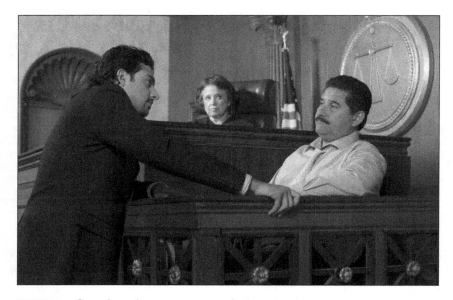

FIGURE 6.4: *Some lay witnesses are more forthcoming than others.*

CASE STUDY

Three armed suspects enter a grocery store around 8 p.m. on a Thursday night. One of the suspects stands by the door and makes sure that no one leaves. Another suspect walks up and down the aisles of the store, forcing the ten shoppers to go to the front of the store and sit by one of the checkout counters. The third suspect takes the manager to the office and orders him to open the safe. When the manager does not readily open the safe, the suspect shoots the manager in the leg.

As an investigator, would you approach the various witnesses in this scenario differently? How would you interact with them? What types of questions would you ask? How would you document the interviews?

Suspects

Suspect interviews vary, depending on the situation and the suspect. Some suspects may be scared, while other will be defiant. Some will want deals before they agree to talk, while others will talk non-stop.

By law, suspects have rights that must be exercised during interviews with law enforcement officers; if these rights are not acknowledged, their statements could be suppressed at trial. Those rights will be addressed in detail in a subsequent Module. Non-law enforcement officers do not have to be concerned about those rights.

Rapport building is important when interviewing suspects. If a suspect believes the investigator is being honest and isn't just trying to get the suspect to confess, there is a better chance of the suspect talking to the investigator. The investigator who tries to intimidate and bully a suspect doesn't get far.

CASE STUDY

At the scene of a car accident, a woman is stabbed and a suspect is apprehended. Witnesses identified the suspect's car as the vehicle that collided with the victim's car. Three witnesses also identified the suspect as the person who stabbed the victim at the scene of the accident. The victim's mother and friends of the victim called the police and reported that the suspect had called them and admitted to stabbing the victim. Investigators also learned that the victim and suspect had been dating for three years and had recently broken up.

How do you approach this interview? How do you build rapport? What types of questions would you ask? What type of non-verbal cues would you be looking for, and how would you use them?

Investigator Bias

As mentioned in Module One, an investigator must be sure not to let his or her personal bias affect the case. Like everyone, investigators form first impressions based on factors including, but not limited to, education, socioeconomic status, employment and sexual orientation. Furthermore, investigators often make a conclusion concerning the victim's truthfulness and degree of cooperation based upon the victim's initial response. However, crimes don't impact all victims the same way. There is no set manner in which a victim will respond.

Example

A 14 year old girl went out on a date and did not return home until three hours after the curfew set by the parents. When she returns home, the parents begin yelling at the victim and tell her that she is going to be grounded for a month. The victim responds by telling her parents that she was sexually assaulted by her date.

If the investigator's initial response is to treat the victim as if she is lying about the sexual assault, the victim may shut down and provide little information. Such a response by the victim may re-enforce the investigator's initial impression. If the victim feels that the investigator doesn't believe her, she may shut down completely, and in some cases become hostile toward the investigator.

Another aspect of investigator bias is identification with the victim. The child who is a victim of sexual or physical abuse, the young female who was brutally sexually assaulted, or the elderly person who had their life's savings taken from them are examples of cases that cause investigators to identify with the victim. This type of bias could lead the investigator to emphasize evidence that leads to the arrest of the suspect, and disregard other pieces of evidence. The investigator may not question any of the information the victim provides, resulting in the investigator losing his objectivity.

Example

The victim is a 95 year old female who gave her life savings to a man to invest in a program that offered a 55% return on an investment. The victim tells the investigator that she has known the suspect since he was a young boy living in her neighborhood.

Based upon what the victim told him, the investigator says that he will make sure the suspect pays all of the victim's money back, and that the suspect will be sent to prison for a long time.

Investigator bias may impact interaction with a suspect in several ways. If the investigator believes that the suspect is guilty, the investigator may not listen to the suspect's explanation, especially if the suspect denies committing the crime. The investigator may not pursue a suspect's alibi or follow-up with witnesses. The bias may go beyond interviews. If the investigator's bias is very strong, he may not pursue forensic analysis that might exonerate the suspect.

With regard to witnesses, the most common type of investigator bias occurs when an investigator does not believe a witness' story. If the investigator doesn't give any credibility to a witness, the investigator may not conduct the appropriate follow-up; for instance, the investigator might not present the witness with a photo lineup. Good investigators do not act immediately based upon those first impressions of victims, suspects or witnesses. Investigators keep the initial impression to themselves, get as much information as possible about the allegations, and then make a conclusion. This helps ensure that the investigator is not acting out of bias. Otherwise, investigator bias can greatly impact a case, because an investigator may emphasize or disregard certain information in order to strengthen his or her point of view.

Summary

Interviewing is a critical component of the investigation process. There are some aspects that apply to interviews of victims, witnesses, and suspects, but there are a number of aspects that are unique to each interview.

The most important aspect of any interview is building rapport, because without rapport, there is no communication. Once communication is established, the investigator must make sure that all of the information obtained during the interview is documented. Investigators must also ensure that information from the interview is not contaminated.

When done effectively, interviews are an invaluable part of the case. When conducted improperly, they can result in a waste of investigative time and possible improper charges against a defendant.

Discussion Questions

1. Discuss how an investigator's use and interpretation of non-verbal communication can be useful during an interview.

2. Explain how rapport can affect interviews of victims, witnesses, and suspects.

3. Discuss how an investigator can help ensure that investigator bias does not affect the interview of suspects accused of the following crimes:

   a. Physical abuse of a baby
   b. Sexual assault of a child
   c. Theft from the elderly

4. Any interview involves the use of open-ended and closed-ended questions. Discuss the advantages of open-ended questions over closed-ended questions when attempting to ascertain what happened during a crime under investigation.

5. Discuss the advantages and disadvantages of the following ways of taking a victim or witness statement:

   a. Digital recording
   b. Investigator compiling a report of the interview
   c. Having the victim/witness write out a statement

Exercises

1. Interview someone you don't know very well concerning one of these topics:

   a. The person's saddest day
   b. The person's happiest day
   c. The person's most memorable day

   Be sure to utilize the principles addressed in this chapter, such as building rapport, asking open-ended questions, and providing feedback. Critique how you conducted the interview.

2. Find an article in a magazine or on the Internet. Critique the interviewer's approach and the answers the interviewee gave. Do you think there was a hidden agenda on the part of either party? Were most of the questions open-ended? Did the interviewer allow the interviewee to answer the questions fully?

3. Go somewhere you can observe people interacting with one another. Observe the following set of groups: man/ man, woman/woman, and man/woman. Concentrate on the individual's non-verbal communication. What messages were being sent? How did the receivers respond to the non-verbal communication? Was there a difference in non-verbal communication among the three groups?

4. As a classroom exercise, break into groups and discuss the various means of non-verbal communication people use every day. Discuss which of the major types of non-verbal communication have the greatest impact and why.

5. Go to **http://crime.about.com/od/current/a/case_news.htm**. Choose a case and determine how investigator bias could impact the investigation. Write a two page paper describing your findings.

Key Terms

Crimes Against Persons: crimes that involved direct physical harm or force to another person.

Crimes Against Property: crimes that involve the destruction, unauthorized use, or theft of another person's possession, including their money, car or home.

Kinesics: study of body movement.

Open-Ended Questions: a type of question that requires a narrative response.

Oculesics: the study of eyes and eye contact in non-verbal communication.

Proxemics: study of social distance and spacing.

Paralanguage: study of speech and its nuances.

Rapport: when two people agree on the means and willingness to communicate.

Structured Interview: a more formal means of interviewing than the traditional interview. Characterized by taking more time, being organized, and asking open-ended questions.

Notes

MODULE 7

Documentation

Key Module Concepts:

- The importance of documenting an investigation

- The various requirements of note taking

- The differences between narrative style and bullet style reporting

- Different methods of documentation

Introduction

As mentioned in previous Modules, the most important lesson concerning **documentation** is taught to rookie police officers during their time at the academy: "If it isn't in your report, it didn't happen." This may be truer in law enforcement than in any other field. Television and movie detectives take few or no notes and don't write reports. Who wants to watch television programs where a great deal of the time the characters are writing reports? However, real life investigators spend a large percentage of their time taking notes and documenting their cases, which makes sense when you consider that the majority of an investigator's time is spent interviewing people.

Taking notes and writing interview reports is only one aspect of documentation. Documentation, as it relates to investigations, also includes descriptions of scenes, review of documents, handling and testing of evidence, surveillance activity, and research. Investigators are constantly asked about their documentation, be it during the course of a criminal investigation, conducting a civil case investigation, or testifying in court. This Module will address three means of documenting information, note-taking, important aspects of report writing, and two general writing formats. This information may not make it more enjoyable to write reports, but it will help make the documentation process a little easier.

The ability to take concise notes and compile excellent reports is one of the most important skills a police officer, law enforcement investigator, or non-law enforcement investigator can possess. For law enforcement investigators, effective report writing is not only critical to the investigative process, but is also an important aspect of professional opportunities, including promotions. An investigator's reports may be read by a number of audiences. As such, the reports form the "first impression" of the investigator. If that first impression is good, positive things can happen. If the first impression is bad, negative things can happen.

Ask Yourself

- *What sort of a first impression can be made from an investigator's notes?*
- *How is documentation used in the trial process?*
- *What documentations styles are most effective, and why?*

In addition to the first impression and negative reputation for the investigator, poor documentation may lead to repercussions, lack of prosecution, a guilty defendant being acquitted, or an innocent person being wrongfully charged. Thorough and complete documentation may also protect an investigator against allegations of police misconduct or criminal activity.

Most investigators did not choose their career path because they enjoy writing reports and consider themselves to be great writers. They see documentation as a necessary evil of the job. The more time investigators are on the job, the more they appreciate the need for clear, concise, and accurate reports.

Example

Example A:

A police department investigator writes a case report that contains many misspellings and incomplete sentences and doesn't flow well, leaving the reader with an incomplete picture of the case investigation. When it comes time to pick a candidate for promotion or a special assignment, that investigator will receive little or no consideration for those positions, because supervisors remember poorly written reports.

Example B:
A police detective is testifying about an interview with a key witness in a case. On the stand, the detective testifies that he didn't put all of the information he received in his report. The report is so poorly written that the defense attorney repeatedly asks the investigator to clarify what was in his report. In the trial closing arguments, the defense attorney tells the jury that the investigating officer did such a poor job of documenting his case that it is unclear what the investigator did or did not do. The attorney then asks the jury what other information was not in the investigator's report that no one knows about and if the jury can, in all conscience, send someone to jail based upon incomplete and unclear information.

Methods of Documenting Information

Taking Notes/Report Writing

The most obvious method of documenting investigative information is writing reports. Note taking and report writing are interlinked. If the investigator doesn't take good notes, it is usually a safe bet that the report will be incomplete. Investigators spend a great deal of their time writing reports. Activity associated with a criminal investigation has to be documented and presented to supervisors and the district attorney's office for filing of criminal charges.

Law enforcement reports are broken into two general categories: administrative reports and investigative reports. **Administrative reports** include injury reports, officer-involved accident reports, proposals, and memorandums. **Investigative reports** include offense reports, supplemental reports, search warrants, arrest warrants, and case summaries. These reports are in a specific, uniform format.

Non-law enforcement investigative reports may or may not be in a specific, uniform format, depending on the organization. Private investigators may have distinctly different formats based upon their perception of what their customers want. Corporate security investigators may have a uniform format so that there is consistency in how information is presented throughout the company.

In law enforcement, the **offense report** (also called the initial report) is the first document completed by the officer or detective handling the scene. The offense report may also be called the crime report or the incident report, but they serve the same purpose: documenting what originally happened. Although all investigative reports are important, the offense report is the most critical, as it documents what the initial officers and/or investigators found upon their response to the scene. The follow-up investigators refer to victim's statements, witness statements, and the responding officers observations throughout the investigation. If the initial information is faulty or incomplete, it will have a negative impact on the follow-up investigation.

Although it may seem relatively insignificant, it is very important to obtain contact information for individuals who were at the scene. Accurate telephone and address information is important for the follow-up investigation. If the telephone/address information was not obtained or is inaccurate, it may cost the follow-up investigators a great deal of investigative time. Another important piece of information is the date of birth for each of the involved parties. It not only helps identify the specific person, i.e. John Smith, but is also an essential piece of information for running criminal histories and other background information.

The narrative section of the offense report is where the responding officer provides the first insight into specifics of a crime. The narrative must not only contain the information that substantiates a criminal act has occurred, but what the specific crime was. It is important that the report contains what information the witnesses and victim provided. Sometimes it is appropriate to paraphrase the information, but other times it may be very important to document the exact wording, as in Examples A and B.

Example

Example A:

A series of bank robberies was committed in a community. During the robberies, the suspect pulled a handgun on a bank teller and said, "Okay, sweetie, it's time to pay the piper."

Such specific verbiage is important in helping investigators determine if the same suspect is committing multiple bank robberies.

Example B:

Officers arrive at the scene of a reported shooting. As the officers are walking up to the door of the residence where the shots reportedly came from, a woman walks out the front door and says, "I didn't mean to shoot him." If the officer writes in his report that the woman said, "I shot him," there is a problem.

The first statement implies that the shooter lacked intent, while the second statement implies the shooter had intent. This has a significant impact on what the shooter is criminally charged with. Additionally, if the woman actually said the first quote and the officer wrote the second quote as coming from the woman, defense counsel will attack the quality of the investigation.

Subsequent to the initial report, investigators will draft supplemental reports, interview reports, search warrants, non-testimonial affidavits, and arrest warrants. All of these documents must be accurate. In addition, any warrant must contain probable cause concerning the alleged crime and where the information came from. Warrants will be covered in more detail in a subsequent chapter.

Supplemental reports are reports that cover investigative activity that occurred subsequent to the initial report. These reports do not restate all of the investigative activity that occurred in the initial report, but rather start with the new information. Each investigator that conducts any investigation subsequent to the initial report should compile a supplemental report. The reports are all tied together by using the same case number, which dispatch provided to patrol when the officers took the initial call.

Some agencies don't require interview reports to be separated from other investigative activity. Other agencies require all interview reports to be separate documents. If the agency records interviews, reference to the interview can be made in the supplemental report rather than compiling a separate report of the interview.

Example

The investigator is conducting a follow-up investigation, which included contacting various potential witnesses and collecting evidence. The investigator tape-recorded each of the interviews, so he need only provide the following information in the supplemental report:

"On March 2, I interviewed James Wilson (date of birth: 10/03/1980). Mr. Wilson provided me with information concerning his relationship with the suspect and the victim. Details concerning that interview can be obtained by reviewing the cassette recording of the interview."

Investigators should not rely completely on the recorded interview. Sometimes batteries fail, the cassette/digital recorder does not work, the interviewee spoke too softly, or some background noise interfered with the clarity of the statements. As a safeguard, the investigator should still take good notes, and document in the report the important aspects of what the interviewee said.

Sometimes investigators go many hours without sleeping or eating anything; they are under enormous pressure to get the reports or warrants completed. There may also be a great deal of activity going on around the investigator while the report is compiled. Investigators will be held to the same standards whether the report is written under the difficult circumstances just described or under the best of conditions.

Digital Recording

A second means of documenting is digital audio- or video-recording. Such recordings include interviews, crime scenes, jail calls, and telephone conversations. Many major police departments have instituted policies stating that all interviews of homicide suspects will be digitally recorded.

Recorded interviews are better than written reports for a number of reasons. They provide a complete documentation of what all parties said and what occurred during the interview. Having the recording also saves the investigator time; the report of the interview doesn't have to contain all of the information that was obtained, because it was all caught on tape. The courts are able to review the video and make rulings on motions concerning the case without having the investigator testify about the entire interview. By the time the case goes to trial, the prosecution may have the investigator give some background, and then introduce the recording into evidence, thus allowing the jury to watch the recording. Digital recordings are easy to copy and can be stored on an investigator's computer, providing easy access to relevant information.

One of the criticisms of recording interview statements is that the interviewee may be uncomfortable talking on video. That discomfort may translate into holding back information. Also, through the interview process, there may be a clarification of information or the interviewee may say things at the end of the interview that were not consistent with what he or she said earlier in the interview. A written report summarizes what was said or done; a digital recording provides all of the dynamics associated with the interview. Some investigators are not comfortable conducting recorded interviews. They are concerned that the recordings subject the investigators to critical scrutiny from the defense attorney concerning how questions were asked, as well as the investigator's reaction to the interviewee's responses.

Recording interviews can also protect the individual against allegations of coercion, misconduct, or perjury.

FIGURE 7.1: *Digital recording is a way to ensure all information is communicated accurately.*

Photography

Another means of documentation used by investigators is photography. Although this topic is covered in detail in another Module, a couple of points are warranted here.

If an investigator addresses some type of evidence in his report, there should be some documentation of that evidence. For example, if the investigator said a footprint was found at the scene of the crime, there should be a casting or picture of the print in evidence. If evidence is referenced in a report, but is not in evidence, defense counsel will raise this issue at trial.

Photographs are important for capturing the scene from an investigative perspective; they can also be of great aid during a trial. A witness' description of a scene that is corroborated by photographs is very helpful to the jury.

Example

A man is charged with sexual assault on a neighborhood boy. During the testimony, the boy described where the assault occurred in the defendant's residence. Pictures of the defendant's residence were introduced into evidence and corroborated the boy's testimony.

CASE STUDY

A woman was found dead in her bathroom. Examination of the body revealed bruises and abrasions consistent with having been beaten with some type of instrument. A diagram of the scene includes a baseball bat. The crime scene photographs contain a picture of a baseball bat in the living room of the victim's residence. The evidence sheet did not list a baseball bat being entered into the evidence bureau.

You are the lead investigator of the case. What would you do to address this issue? What are the potential issues associated with this situation?

Note Taking Methods

Notes are the foundation for reports. If notes are incomplete or confusing, the report will be also. Taking notes is an acquired skill, honed by repetition and utilizing these skills:

- Prepare to take notes by listing the following information in the upper left-hand corner of the first page:

  - the date and time

  - location of the interview

  - individuals present at the interview

- Number the pages

- Don't write your notes in sentence format, as this is very time-consuming. Unless you are very skilled, you won't be able to keep up with the interviewee. Instead, write in the **bullet-style**, meaning you are only writing down the important aspect.

  Example: If the interviewee said he was at his home and Sam came over at 10:00 a.m., your notes would be "At home: Sam came over at 10 a.m."

- There is nothing wrong with using abbreviations, as long as you know what the abbreviations stand for

- Don't write down the questions. What is important is what the person is telling you.

- Even if there are two interviewers, both should take notes. This helps increase the likelihood that all of the information will be recorded. Taking notes holds true even if the interview is being recorded. Sometimes equipment breaks down, or the quality of the recording may be poor.

- After you have completed the interview, go over your notes and edit. If you are writing your notes in the bullet-style (meaning just the important aspect), it is important to go over them immediately after the interview.

- Constantly work on your listening and note-taking skills. This will help you gather the information the interviewee is providing.

- If the interviewee said something that you are quoting in your notes, use quotation marks

  Example: He said, "I was fed up with his lying to me and I shot him."

- Keep your notes, even after the investigation is completed

During court proceedings, the court will allow you to **refresh your memory** by looking at your notes. In many jurisdictions, your notes are part of discovery (to be discussed in another Module) and copies must be provided to defense counsel.

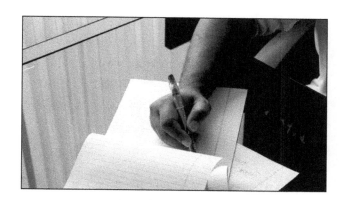

FIGURE 7.2: *Effective investigators require thorough notes to compile reports that are admissible as trial evidence.*

Important Aspects of Report Writing

Reports need to be completed in a timely manner, which most departments interpret as being within 24 hours of obtaining the information. Most investigators try to write their reports within hours of the event. In addition to the information being available to other individuals associated with the investigation, the information is still fresh in the investigator's mind. Another reason for writing the report in a timely manner is something that many students can identify with. With the passage of time and the approach of a deadline, the writer may be hurried to complete the report. The writer is not able to take as much time to think about effective means of conveying information, edit the document, or organize the document.

The ultimate goal of effective report writing is to convey complete and accurate information to the reader. Effective report writing provides a picture of the event being recorded. It also allows the reader to form a conclusion that is consistent with what the writer is trying to convey. An effective report is concise, accurate, and grammatically correct.

Above everything else, accurately recording information is the most important component of documentation. The initial offense report, contains the first information available about a case, and will be constantly referenced during the course of the investigation. Misstatements of facts can result in a guilty person not being held accountable or an innocent person being convicted. Incorrect telephone numbers or addresses impact investigative time. Failing to document times and statements can greatly impact a case.

Example

In the initial report of a child abuse case, the responding officer failed to document the suspect's statement about the suspect seeing a bruise on the victim's forehead. This became a critical part of the prosecution's case because the child did not have any external signs of an injury. Autopsy revealed a subcutaneous bleed and an impression of an adjusting screw from animal grooming shears. The prosecution argued that the only way the defendant could know about the bruise being on the forehead was if she caused it, since the injury was not visible on the child's forehead.

Secondly, documentation should be concise. Some investigators get caught up in using either police jargon or "big words." Investigative documentation is meant to convey facts so that the reader understands what occurred. With that in mind, investigators should write in short sentences, using common verbiage. Big words or police jargon take away from the purpose of the documentation.

Avoid writing, "The officer alighted from his uniform patrol vehicle and confronted the alleged suspect." More effective wording would be, "The officer exited his patrol car and contacted Mr. Smith."

Reports should be in the **first person**, meaning the person who is doing the action, such as, "I arrived at the scene at 9 a.m." The other important grammatical aspect is writing in the **active voice** rather than the **passive voice**. Grammatically, active voice means that the subject is doing the action. In passive voice, the subject is no longer active. Active voice makes it easy to understand who did what. It is also less wordy and cumbersome.

As stated in an earlier Module, an investigator must avoid being biased in his investigation. This also applies to an investigator's written reports. Reports should be unbiased, and present only facts, not opinions. For instance, an investigator should not document that "It was obvious that the suspect was lying." The investigator can get the point across without making a conclusion by writing "The suspect hesitated before answering, did not have any eye contact with me, and was squirming around in her seat."

It is important that the investigator set the stage when writing a report. Setting the stage means that the reader learns when and where the action took place.

Example

"At approximately 10:30 p.m. on June 10, 2010, I met with the suspect at the police department."

In the above sentence, the stage is set for the investigator to tell the reader what happened.

After setting the stage, the investigator addresses what happened. After completing this portion of the report, the investigator ends the report by providing information as to where the investigation will go next.

Information that is beneficial to the defendant must be provided to the defense. Failure to provide this information could result in sanctions against the officer, including dismissal of the case and criminal charges against the investigator. The rule of thumb is, "Everything an investigator learns during the course of the investigation should be documented."

Example

During the course of the investigation, a witness came forward and told the investigator that the defendant had been with the witness during the commission of the crime. The investigator decided not to include this information in his report because the witness had a criminal history, including charges of perjury. The investigator also knew that the witness was married to the defendant's sister and would probably lie to protect the defendant.

When the information came to light during the trial, the court dismissed the case against the defendant. The detective was demoted.

Writing Formats

There are two basic writing formats: the narrative style and the bullet style.

In the **narrative style**, the information is in the format found in many books. The narrative style tells a story, usually in a chronological order.

Example

"At approximately 11:30 p.m., I arrived at 1234 South Main Street after a dispatch call about shots fired. At the residence I contacted Mrs. Smith, who told me that she had shot her husband. Mrs. Smith also told me that she had been married to her husband for ten years and that he was a chronic abuser of Mrs. Smith and her children. Mrs. Smith then showed me where Mr. Smith was and where Mrs. Smith had put the gun."

The law enforcement investigator's obligation in the written report is to convey information that is associated with the case, not to entertain the reader. It is also important that information obtained is understandable. The narrative style is a problem for some investigators in that it requires the information to be broken up into sentences and paragraphs. Additionally, it isn't always easy to find a specific instance in a narrative report. Some investigators also complain that they don't want to keep starting sentences the same way, such as "And then she told me."

The bullet style emphasizes the information that was obtained. Rather than writing in paragraphs and sentences, the writer uses an introductory sentence and then lists the information under that category.

The bullet style of reporting is subject based, not chronologically based. It is much easier to find information in the report, and the investigator doesn't need to constantly look for new ways to start sentences. Most importantly, it is an easy way to write a report based on the interview notes.

Example

Mrs. Smith provided me with the following information concerning her relationship with her husband:

- They have been married for ten years

- Mr. Smith "chronically" abused Mrs. Smith and her children

- Mr. Smith threatened to kill Mrs. Smith if she ever tried to leave.

When the investigator wants to change topics, he writes a new introductory sentence and lists information under that sentence.

Example

Mrs. Smith provided me with the following information concerning what happened today:

- Mr. and Mrs. Smith got up around 7 a.m. and Mrs. Smith fixed breakfast

- Neither Mr. nor Mrs. Smith worked that day and planned to do some things around the house

- Mr. Smith did not like the way his eggs were prepared, so he started yelling at Mrs. Smith and threw the plate of eggs across the table at Mrs. Smith

Organization Considerations

Whether the investigator is a detective for a police agency or an investigator for a private company, organizational skills are very important. Failure to start and maintain an organized investigation could negatively impact the case:

- Duplicity in effort: If investigators don't document what they did or didn't do, someone else may do the same work

- Lack of direction: Someone needs to be in charge and coordinate the investigation

- Lack of communication: Investigators need to know who is handling the various aspects of the investigation. Without communication, aspects of the investigation will be missed.

- Lack of organization: If the material is not organized efficiently, investigators waste time looking for information

A well-organized case helps facilitate a complete investigation and provide a professional product. It also helps ensure that all information is provided to the prosecution.

How to Organize the Case

There are two aspects when talking about case organization: the actual investigation and the organization of the case material. Both are critical to an effective investigation. The organizational aspects of the actual investigation are critical, for without an organized approach information will not be obtained or may be overlooked.

The Physical Investigation

The first step in organizing a case is to determine everyone's role in the investigation. In law enforcement cases, a lead investigator is assigned to oversee the investigation and receives supervisory support from a sergeant. In non-law enforcement investigations, there may be only one investigator who has to report to a supervisor. In either case, the lead investigator must determine what type of case is being investigated, what type of support is needed, and establish an initial approach.

Some agencies have a protocol for handling cases. For example, detectives working sexual assault cases know that the first stage of the investigation requires determining what type of assault occurred and whether the suspect is still in the area. If the assault went further than sexual touching, the victim's clothing must be secured, and the victim must be taken to a hospital for a physical examination. Many homicide divisions have a "homicide notebook," a three-ring binder that has labeled tabs for various sections associated with the case. There is also a written protocol on how to handle the case. Private companies may not have the luxury of a written investigative protocol. In such cases, the investigator needs to step back from the situation for a moment and determine the approach.

Once the lead investigator has been established, he or she determines the roles of other investigators and how to initially proceed. The investigation then goes to the next organizational consideration: communication.

Communication is a critical component of any investigation. If investigators don't inform other investigators or supervisors of what has been done, aspects of the investigation may be overlooked, or there may be duplicity of effort. Regular meetings should be established and everyone associated with the investigation should participate. The meetings should discuss what has been done, determine what is to be done, and establish a time frame for those tasks.

Even the best investigator needs to confer with other people to ensure every aspect of the investigation is completed, and to discuss problem areas and interpret the evidence.

Once all of the tasks are completed, one last meeting should be conducted to ensure the investigation is complete.

FIGURE 7.3: *Investigative documents should be well organized for easy retrieval.*

Document Organization

During the course of any investigation, documents, pieces of evidence, photographs, and digital recordings may be obtained. If an organizational plan is not in place at the beginning of the investigation, it is often difficult to organize material as the investigation proceeds. There are a number of methods that can help keep an investigation organized from the onset.

Use either a three-ring binder or folders to keep the case organized. Set up general sections in the three-ring binder, or label the folders so that when information is obtained it can be placed in the appropriate section:

- Initial Offense Report

- Supplemental Reports

- Witness List

- Statements

- Evidence

- Assignment Sheet

- Activity Log

- Criminal Histories

- Suspect Information

- Diagrams

- Warrants

The sections may vary depending on the case being investigated. Crimes against persons may include medical information, pathology/forensics, and serious bodily injury forms. Other types of offenses may have fewer sections. All cases should be organized in such a manner that anyone working the case can readily find and properly place information.

Activity Log

Keep a log of all activities that occur during the course of an investigation. Get in the habit of entering the activity soon after the activity is completed.

Example

June 1, 2011

Called and spoke with John Stevens (date of birth 10/23/1984). He provided background information concerning the defendant.

June 2, 2011

Reviewed the collected property in the Property Bureau

Witness List

Maintain an ongoing witness list. After you contact potential witnesses, put them on the list. Provide their contact information and a general summary of their testimony.

Name: John Stevens (date of birth: 10/23/1984)

Address: 1234 South Jellison Avenue, Midtown

Telephone Number: 356-698-3618

Summary: Will testify to being with the defendant on the night of the shooting.

This helps keep track of who has been contacted and what they provide to the case.

Evidence Summary

List the property seized, whether it was sent to the lab, and the results of any testing.

- Shirt from defendant

  a. Seized from defendant on 01/23/2010

  b. Placed into property bureau on 01/23/2010

  c. Submitted for lab analysis on 02/03/2010

  d. Analysis shows DNA of victim was on the shirt

- Firearm taken from defendant's car

  a. Seized on 01/23/2010

  b. Placed into property bureau on 01/23/2010

  c. Submitted for analysis on 02/03/2010

  d. Analysis showed that firearm was in working order and ballistics showed it was the gun that fired the bullet recovered from the victim

Example

An investigator for a major corporation was asked to investigate the disappearance of twelve computers from the home office of the company. The CEO of the company instructed the Corporate Security Director to assign as many people as needed to conduct the investigation. The Corporate Security Director assigned John Long as the lead investigator and Brian Shea as the secondary.

On the first day, the director met with Mr. Long and Mr. Shea and provided an overview of the situation. Mr. Long and Mr. Shea provided suggestions on how they thought the investigation should start. Once everyone was in agreement, Mr. Long and Mr. Shea began their investigation.

Pictures were taken of the location from which the computers had been taken, and the scene was processed. Mr. Shea checked the security cameras and the security sign-in sheet while Mr. Long began conducting interviews. Each interview was recorded.

Example

At the end of the day, Mr. Long and Mr. Shea met with the director and informed him of the day's activity. Mr. Long obtained a three-ring binder and organized the binder into sections. The binder had tabbed sections for investigators' activity, evidence, witness list, interviews, criminal histories, and suspect information. As new information came in, Mr. Long was responsible for making sure the new information was placed in the appropriate section.

After the first three days of the investigation, Mr. Long and Mr. Shea met with the director and provided him with an overview of what had been obtained. The director, Mr. Long, and Mr. Shea discussed the progress and future of the case.

Over the following two days, Mr. Long and Mr. Shea completed the tasks discussed during the latest meeting. A suspect had been developed and interviewed. Although the suspect denied any involvement in the theft, Mr. Long thought there was sufficient evidence to charge the suspect.

Mr. Long and Mr. Shea took the completed investigative binder to the local law enforcement agency and presented their case. The police department agreed that there was sufficient evidence to criminally charge the defendant. A copy of the investigative binder was turned over to the police department. The police department executed a search warrant on the defendant's residence, added that information to the investigative binder, and turned the binder over to the District Attorney's office for filing.

Summary

Documentation, which includes note taking, report writing, crime scene sketches, photographs, the review of documents, and the handling/testing of evidence, is a critical aspect of any investigation. An investigator can conduct a very professional and thorough investigation, but if it is not documented well, or if it is poorly organized, the case may be lost.

Documentation is not only critical for the filing and subsequent trial of a case; it is also important for career advancement. District Attorneys and investigative supervisors put a premium on an investigator's ability to provide a complete, concise, and accurate product.

All investigations require the ability of an investigator to take detailed notes and to transfer those notes into concise and comprehensive reports. The investigative reports are the basis for follow-up investigations, administrative actions, and trials. If the notes are incorrect, the report will be incorrect, and any follow-up will be impacted.

Reports must be written in first person, use active voice, and must be void of any opinion. The best reports are a compilation of facts presented in a manner that allows the reader to have a clear understanding of what was done or found.

While some agencies still write in the narrative style, many agencies have moved to the bullet style of writing. The bullet style is easier to read, and it is easier to find specific information because it is organized by topic.

Photography and digital recording are also important aspects of documenting an investigation. There is no uniformity as to mandatory use of photography or digital recording. A major advantage of digital recording is that there is no question as to what was said or done. The recording speaks for itself. With that benefit comes the burden of making sure everything was done correctly, as the recording is available for everyone to critique.

Organization of a case is also critical to avoid duplicity of work and to ensure that everything is covered. Major cases should be organized in such a manner that any investigator, supervisor, or attorney can readily find the information that is needed. In addition to being very functional, it presents a professional product.

Discussion Questions

1. Discuss the importance of proper documentation as it relates to:

    a. A trial
    b. Private investigator cases
    c. Corporate security cases

2. Discuss the various ways that an investigator can help ensure that information obtained from victims and witnesses is not contaminated.

3. Discuss the importance of organizing your case from an investigation perspective and from a presentation perspective.

4. Discuss the positive and negative aspects of the "narrative style" and the "bullet style" of report writing.

5. Discuss the various means of documenting a witness interview using digital recording. What are the negative aspects of digitally recording an interview or having the witness write out his own statement?

Exercises

1. Break the class into teams of two. Have one student "interview" the other student about his background and why the interviewee wants to go into criminal justice. The interviewer should take handwritten notes during the process. After a ten to fifteen-minute interview, change roles. At the end of the exercise, hold a classroom discussion about the note-taking process.

2. Write a report addressing what happened during last weekend. Be sure to write in "first person" and "set the stage" as to what you are writing about. Be descriptive, and determine what is important. Compare your reports with other students.

3. Conduct an interview of a family member. Confine the interview to one topic, such as an embarrassing moment or contact with law enforcement. Be sure to take notes and write the report using the bullet style.

4. Take the information obtained in Exercise #1 and write it in a "bullet-style" format.

Key Terms

Active Voice: a type of writing in which the subject of the sentence is performing the action. Example: The investigator met with the victims.

Administrative Reports: reports that are associated with a department or business. Examples: proposals, memoranda, disciplinary reports.

Bullet-Style: a writing style that emphasizes listing of information.

Documentation: the recording, by writing or some other means, of the actions that occurred during the course of an investigation.

First Person: the grammatical form by which the subject of the sentence refers to himself. Example: I spoke with the witnesses.

Interview Reports: reports pertaining to the interview of witnesses, victims, and suspects.

Investigative Reports: reports pertaining to the action taken by an investigator during the course of an investigation.

Narrative Style: a writing style characterized by telling a story, usually in a chronological order.

Non-Testimonial Evidence: non-verbal testimonial evidence associated with a suspect. Examples include: blood, physical characteristics, and injuries.

Offense Reports: the initial report law enforcement officers take during the course of an investigation.

Passive Voice: the grammatical style in which the subject of the sentence is the recipient of the action, rather than the performer. Example: The books were put on the shelf by the librarian.

Refresh Your Memory: in the judicial system, the procedure by which a witness can refer to previously written reports of the witness before answering the posed question.

Supplemental Reports: law enforcement reports that are compiled subsequent to the "offense report."

Notes

MODULE 8
Forensics

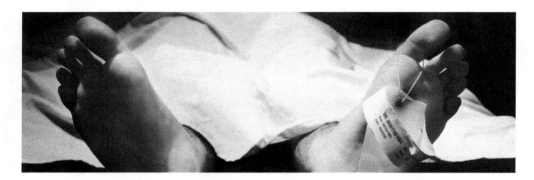

Key Module Concepts:

- The importance of forensic science in investigations

- Different specialties within the forensic science field

- The differences between class characteristics and individual characteristics

- The importance of the chain of custody when admitting evidence into trial

- The significance of certain types of evidence, such as fingerprints, DNA, and fibers

Introduction

Forensic science, often referred to simply as "forensics," is the application of various sciences to answer questions associated with the legal system. Forensics is centered on the concept of helping find out what occurred. The forensic pathologist who conducts the autopsy of a murder victim; the investigator who investigates a case where a victim was found dead in his bedroom; and the firearms analyst who attempts to ascertain whether the bullet found in the victim's body came from the defendant's gun are utilizing forensic science to help determine what occurred. Forensic science has application in both civil and criminal cases.

The use of forensics in investigations and prosecutions is so prevalent today, it is hard to imagine a time when that wasn't the case. From a historical perspective, the role of forensics in criminal investigations is relatively new. The first court to convict a defendant by fingerprint evidence was in 1892; this type of evidence was not used as a means of identifying criminals until 1903. One of the first uses of DNA in a criminal case in the United States occurred in 1987. The increased use of forensics resulted in the standardization of police procedures and more scientific evaluation of evidence. Today's investigators must strive to balance good investigative procedures/techniques with the use of forensics.

Thanks in large part to such shows as "CSI" and "Forensic Files," many people have some understanding of forensic science and its application to criminal investigations. Public perception is such that jurors expect forensic science to play a major role in criminal trials. This perception is called the CSI Syndrome. The perception sometimes results in juries placing a high burden on prosecutors to use forensic evidence.

Ask Yourself

- *What is the importance of forensics to a criminal investigation?*
- *What are the strengths and weaknesses of forensic evidence to any given case?*
- *How does forensic science help ensure that the guilty are prosecuted and the innocent are exonerated?*

Example

In a criminal trial, an investigator testifies that bloodstains were found at a crime scene. Because of the television and movie portrayal of bloodstain analysis, jurors expect investigators to be able to identify all of the blood at the scene and tie the blood to the suspect. In reality, some of the blood is "uninterpretable," or there is such a small quantity that the serologist can't obtain a DNA profile.

A jury is informed that hairs were found at the scene of a crime. The jurors expect the hair to be tied to a specific person. In reality, if the hair doesn't have a bulb, a DNA profile cannot be identified. Hairs without bulbs can only be microscopically compared to other hairs and determine whether they have the same class characteristics.

Some of the more common and often used applications of forensics will be discussed in the following sections.

Forensic Specialties

Prior to the late nineteenth and early twentieth centuries, investigators relied on investigative techniques, contacts in the community, witnesses, interviews of suspects, and a degree of luck. Today investigators rely on a wide range of forensic specialties.

Forensic Pathology
The postmortem examination of a deceased person to establish cause, manner, and time of death.

Forensic Anthropology
The postmortem examination of human remains to help identify the deceased. Forensic Anthropology may also help establish time and cause of death. By reviewing human remains, the forensic anthropologist can determine race, sex, approximate height, old injuries, and even some illnesses.

Forensic Odontology

The examination of teeth is often a helpful means of identifying a person. In addition to identifying remains, a forensic odontologist can compare bite marks on a victim and determine whether the bite marks match a suspect.

Forensic Toxicology

Toxicologists can ascertain what levels of drugs or poisons are in the body of the deceased. Toxicologists can also provide information concerning toxic levels, symptoms associated with various drugs and poisons, and estimated time of death after having the drug/poison injected, ingested, or absorbed into the bloodstream.

Forensics in the Courtroom

For lab analysis to be admissible in court, the procedures and techniques used during evidence collection and in the lab must rely on a firm scientific foundation that meets the standards imposed by the court.

In addition to the accepted procedures and techniques, the prosecution has to demonstrate to the court that the evidence was handled in such a manner that the evidence was not contaminated or subject to misinterpretation.

Example

An item of bloody clothing was seized at a crime scene. If the investigator wasn't wearing gloves when the item was seized, the investigator's DNA may transfer onto the item.

If the item was still wet when the investigator placed the item in an evidence bag, the stain could be transferred to another part of the piece of evidence, resulting in a bloodstain pattern that is subject to misinterpretation.

Locard's Principle

Locard's Principle, previously mentioned in Module Three, is one of the core principles associated with forensics. Although some investigators may not know the principle by name, every investigator is aware that suspects leave and take something from every crime scene.

The suspect who mugs a victim may leave hairs, fibers, DNA or other evidence. Just as importantly, the suspect may take hair, fibers, DNA or other evidence from the victim. The evidence that is left or removed is called **trace evidence**, which is evidence associated with two people or things coming into contact with one another. **Transfer evidence** is a type of trace evidence in which evidence from one source is transferred to another source.

Examples of Trace and Transfer Evidence:

- A car collides with another car and leaves the scene of the accident. Paint from the striking vehicle may be left on the vehicle that was struck (transfer evidence), or flakes of paint may be left on the ground (trace evidence). Paint from the vehicle that was struck may be transferred to the striking car (transfer evidence). Parts of the striking vehicle may be left at the scene (trace evidence), or pieces from the struck vehicle may adhere to the striking vehicle (transfer evidence).

- A struggle ensues during the course of an armed robbery. The suspect grabs the victim's shirt, tearing it. The suspect repeatedly hits the victim in the face, breaking the victim's nose. Fibers from the victim's shirt may adhere to the suspect's clothing, blood from the victim may get on the suspect's clothing, or the victim may have injured the suspect during the struggle and have the suspect's DNA under his fingernails.

Investigators do not always find trace evidence. That doesn't mean trace evidence does not exist, only that it was not found, or that today's technology is not sophisticated enough to locate all of the trace evidence associated with a crime. With the advances in forensics, the ability to find additional trace evidence will be enhanced.

Example

There was a time that bloodstain evidence was limited to what an investigator could observe with the naked eye. With the advent of a chemical called luminol, investigators can find areas that contained blood and had been cleaned up, or traces of blood that were not visible to the naked eye.

Class and Individual Characteristics

When comparing one piece of evidence to another, the comparison may reveal class characteristics, individual characteristics, or no characteristics. **Class characteristics** means that the items of evidence being compared have measurable features in common, but it cannot be determined whether the items came from the same source. The same **individual characteristics** show that one piece of evidence is measurably certain to have come from the same source as the piece of evidence with which it is being compared.

Example

A recovered bullet from the victim's body was compared to a bullet that was test-fired in the lab. The class characteristics may be that the bullets are of the same caliber, weight, and general appearance. An example of individual characteristics would be that the striation marks on the test-fired bullet match the striation marks on the recovered bullet. The examiner could conclude, based on the individual characteristics, that the bullets were fired from the same gun. If the examiner only found class characteristics, the examiner's conclusion would be that the bullets may have been fired from the same gun. Such conclusions are important during the course of the investigation, but may be critical in the trial phase. If the jury is given evidence that has only class characteristics, the jury may conclude that such evidence is not sufficient to convict the defendant. If the evidence has individual characteristics, the jury may more readily convict the defendant.

Evidence Contamination

Proper documentation and preservation of evidence is critical. Forensic evidence may be handled by a number of people after the initial identification and preservation. After the initial seizing of the evidence, the evidence may be handled by a fingerprint analyst, a DNA analyst, and/or a hair and fiber analyst. As with other types of evidence, every time a piece of forensic evidence is examined, the individual who conducts the examination must ensure that the chain of custody (or chain of evidence) is properly documented and followed. The chain of evidence is usually documented in two ways: an evidence form and the packaging associated with the evidence. When an investigator first packages a piece of evidence, she fills out an evidence form (also known as evidence report/property tag form). The evidence form contains information pertinent to the case: where the item was found, the number of items associated with the evidence, and how many items were seized. The evidence is placed in a property bureau, and a copy of the evidence sheet accompanies the property. Each time an individual takes the evidence out of the property bureau, that individual must sign the evidence sheet. See Exhibit F, Property Sign-Out Sheet form in the Resources section, for a sample form.

Example

A suspect fired a gun during the robbery of a convenience store. Investigators recovered a spent bullet from the wall of the convenience store. The recovered bullet had gone through a customer at the convenience store prior to being lodged in the wall. A handgun was recovered from a dumpster a block away from the convenience store. The investigators at the scene obtain, label, and package the spent bullet and handgun, and then send the items to the property bureau.

A ballistics expert checks the packages containing the gun and bullet out of the property bureau. The ballistics expert opens the packaging, careful not to disturb the original seal. After the ballistics expert makes his examination, the evidence is placed back in the packaging and the expert seals the new opening with evidence tape.

The ballistics expert then places his initials and the date on the new evidence tape.

Making the entries on the evidence sheet and properly labeling the packaging that contains the evidence establishes the chain of custody. The importance of establishing the chain of evidence and being able to testify as to what happened with the evidence is to negate any allegation that the evidence was contaminated. If the court determines that a piece of evidence is contaminated, the court could determine that the evidence is inadmissible in the court proceedings or determine that the **weight**, or significance, of the evidence is compromised.

Investigative Stages Relating to Forensic Evidence

There are five stages relating to forensic evidence:

- Finding the evidence

- Recording the evidence

- Collecting the evidence

- Protecting the evidence

- Analyzing the evidence

Finding the Evidence

Finding the evidence can be the most challenging of these stages, as what constitutes evidence on any particular case may not be apparent. This is true for all types of crimes. In addition to not being able to readily identify what is evidence in association with a particular crime, the investigators may be under various time constraints to release the crime scene. The investigator's constant challenge in this phase of the investigation is to conduct a thorough yet timely search. If evidence is found after a crime scene is released, the evidence may be compromised or ruled inadmissible. However, it is better to have the evidence suppressed at a later hearing that to not have the evidence at all.

Example 	Investigators working an embezzlement case conduct a search of a residence. They collect a desktop computer, various ledgers, and written documents. After the investigators released the scene, a witness meets with detectives and provides them with a laptop computer that she claims was found underneath the mattress in the defendant's residence. The laptop computer contained relevant information concerning the suspect's alleged criminal activity. At trial, defense counsel will contend that the investigators conducted a thorough search of the house and did not find the laptop; therefore, the witness must be planting the evidence. Defense counsel may also contend that since investigators did not find the computer in the defendant's residence, there is nothing tying the defendant to the laptop. The court will then have to make a ruling about the admissibility of the laptop computer.

While crime scenes may be released in a short amount of time, in some cases, investigators may control the crime scene for an extended period of time. The court may have to determine if the scene must be released in a "reasonable amount of time" if the defendant alleges that investigators' control of the crime scene is causing an undue hardship on the defendant. An example of such a case is an investigation involving the seizure of the defendant's bank accounts, computers, and written documents.

Recording the Evidence

We have previously discussed the importance of sketching, photographing, videotaping, and taking notes. The importance of note-taking and documentation of the scene and evidence warrants bears repeating.

During a trial, an investigator may ask that he be allowed to review his notes to "refresh" his recollection. Good notes will help ensure that the investigator provides accurate testimony concerning what was found at the scene.

Documentation of the scene, especially in the form of photographs, is essential to communication. Photographs of weapons, injuries, and the scene convey an image that words cannot fully describe, and ensure that everyone involved has the same image. Photographs can be enlarged and made into court exhibits that help relate the scene to the jury.

Collecting the Evidence

Evidence found at the scene must be properly collected. Some evidence is very fragile and can be lost or compromised if not collected properly. Footprints, tire tracks, and fingerprints are especially subject to deterioration. Taking clear and detailed photographs is essential to aid in subsequent examination. Casts of footprints and tire tracks may contain class or individual characteristics that help solve the crime.

Example

The victim told investigators that she was taken to a secluded area off of the main highway and sexually assaulted. The victim took the investigators to the area, where they found partial tire tracks and footprints. Close-up photos of the footprints and tire tracks were taken, as well as plaster castings. When investigators pinpointed a suspect, they obtained his shoes and took impressions of the tires on his truck. Both sets of prints matched the impressions found at the scene.

The most important aspects of collecting evidence are to avoid contamination of evidence and to ensure that fragile evidence is collected and packaged properly. Sometimes contamination can occur with the best of intentions. An investigator is wearing gloves and using tweezers to pick up a hair found on the carpet and is painstakingly trying to place the hair into an evidence tube. Without thinking, the investigator blows on the hair to get it to fall into the tube. The result may be a compromised piece of evidence.

Protecting the Evidence

Always make sure evidence is properly bagged and sealed. There are a wide range of containers to ensure the evidence is properly packaged. Moist evidence should be dried before packaging and put into containers that are not airtight. As a rule of thumb, all items containing blood should be packaged in paper bags. Hair samples should be placed on a clean piece of paper, folded, and placed in an envelope.

As addressed earlier, once the items have been placed into a container, the container should be sealed with evidence tape. The packaging should contain the case number, the item number (that corresponds to the property sheet), the date and time that the item was seized, and the location. The packaging should also contain the officer's initials.

Subsequent to the initial seizing of evidence, investigators and/or attorneys may determine that they want to review evidence. In such cases, only one person should handle the evidence. The individual handling the evidence must wear gloves and ensure that only one piece of evidence is examined at a time. The item should be placed on a clean surface, usually butcher-block paper, and examined. After reviewing the item, the item should be resealed and the butcher-block paper replaced before another item is examined. It is also recommended that new gloves are worn prior to examining another item, especially if the item may involve DNA evidence.

Analyzing the Evidence

In this stage, the evidence is analyzed and the relevance to the case is determined. Different types of forensics can provide valuable information. Analyzed evidence may include: hair and fibers, DNA, impressions such as tire tracks or footprints, bite marks, ballistics, soil, and tool marks. Often analysis of the evidence requires specialized equipment and highly trained scientists. Investigators should keep in mind that analysts are not always able to give a definitive answer concerning all pieces of evidence. The evidence may have been compromised before seizure, may be too small a sample to be analyzed, or analysis may be inconclusive.

Signs of Death

Rigor mortis, livor mortis, and algor mortis can help the forensic pathologist determine the approximate time of death. **Rigor mortis** is the process by which various muscles stiffen after death. **Livor mortis** (also known as lividity) is the process following death in which the blood begins to settle in parts of the body that are closest to the ground due to gravitational pull, causing reddish or dark areas on the skin. **Algor mortis** is the process by which the body decreases to room temperature after death. While these three factors are helpful in establishing a window into the time of death, they can also be influenced by temperature, location of the body, and other dynamics, thus determining the exact time of death impossible.

Autopsy

The forensic pathologist can provide a great deal of information concerning **cause of death** and means of death by conducting an **autopsy**. The forensic pathologist must determine if the individual died as a result of a medical condition, suicide, accident, or homicide. By examining the body via autopsy, the forensic pathologist may able to explain the dynamics surrounding the victim's death, provide an approximate time of death, and provide information concerning the weapon used to cause death. Autopsies are divided into several phases. The first is the **gross examination**, in which the forensic examiner examines the exterior of the decedent. The second phase is an examination of the internal organs of the body. The third is the **cranial examination**, which is the examination of the brain. The final stage is **toxicology**, which determines if there is anything unusual about the levels of any substance in the decedent's bloodstream.

Types of Wounds

Forensic pathologists may encounter a number of different types of wounds that indicate whether the victim suffered a physical assault.

- **Abrasion**: an injury in which skin is scraped off

- **Concussion**: a serious brain injury caused by a strong blow to the head

- **Contusion**: a bruise

- **Fracture**: a break or crack in a bone

- **Laceration**: a cut

- **Subdural Hematoma**: bleeding in the brain

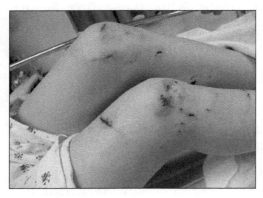

FIGURE 8.1: *Wounds can help a pathologist figure out if the victim was assaulted.*

Injuries associated with gunshot wounds can provide information concerning the approximate distance the shooter was from the victim, entry and exit wounds, and the caliber of gun used.

Defensive wounds, which are usually found on the victim's hands and the inside portion of the victim's forearms, help establish that the victim was attempting to shield himself rather than being an aggressor.

Fingerprints

Fingerprints are still the major source of identifying individuals. Fingerprints can be left when a person has something on his hands and leaves a mark. Examples would be fingers that have blood, ink, or paint on them. Fingerprints can also be left if the suspect touches a soft surface, leaving an impression, or when the oil on the suspect's hand comes in contact with a surface and leaves a pattern. Contrary to popular belief, fingerprints are not always readily apparent or found at a scene. Humidity and the individual's oils play a major role in whether or not a fingerprint is left at the scene. The surface that is touched also impacts the likelihood that a print is left or could be lifted.

Today, some agencies use computer scanning to take fingerprints, rather than the traditional ink method. In the scan method, fingerprint images are submitted electronically using a scanning device. This does not require the use of ink and if the image is not suitable, the person taking the prints can delete and re-take the prints.

The FBI's **Integrated Automated Fingerprint Identification System (IAFIS)** is one of the largest fingerprint databases in the world; it is able to search through hundreds of thousands of fingerprints in less than a second.

If a print recovered from a crime scene is put into IAFIS, the agency that submitted the original print will be provided with possible matches. A fingerprint expert still needs to actually compare the "hits" to the unknown print to determine there is a match. The examiner compares the **arches**, **loops**, and **whorls** of the two prints to determine if the prints match.

Firearms

Ballistics is the analysis of bullets and bullet impacts. Ballistics experts analyze firearms and ammunition to determine if a certain model or caliber was used in the commission of a crime. When a gun is fired, there are several pieces of potential evidence: the gun, the bullet, and the casing. Not only can these pieces of evidence potentially tie the bullet to the gun; fingerprint and DNA evidence may tie the gun and/or the bullet to the shooter. **Gunshot residue testing (GSR)** can help establish that the suspect recently shot a firearm, or was in close proximity when a gun was fired. Three aspects of the firearm are examined: the striations on the bullet, the firing pin, and the rifling (the latter if a handgun was used). The **striations** are also referred to as lands and grooves, and are marks that the inside of the barrel leave on the bullet when it is fired. By examining the lands and grooves and the "twist" of the bullet (the direction the bullet rotates when it comes out of the barrel), the examiner can often determine the make and model of the firearm that was used to shoot the bullet.

Example

Two men got into an altercation; one of the men pulled a handgun and shot the other. The bullet went through the victim's arm and lodged in the wall.

Investigators recovered the gun from the suspect and the spent round from the wall. The firearms expert took the recovered gun and shot a bullet from it. The test-round was then compared to the bullet recovered from the scene. Microscopically, the striations (lands and groove) of the two bullets matched. Both bullets had a right-hand twist. Based upon the analysis, the expert would testify that the gun recovered from the suspect shot the bullet recovered at the scene.

In addition to determining the general condition of the firearm and whether the firearm is functional, the analyst can determine the amount of pressure needed to pull the trigger.

A casing is the metal jacket that contains the bullet and ammunition. The analyst can determine if casings found at the scene are consistent with live ammunition, or casings, recovered from the defendant or found at the defendant's residence. (This type of evidence would show class characteristics rather than individual characteristics.) Spent casings, meaning casings of bullets that have been fired, can provide valuable information by examining the firing pin impression left on the spent round. Analysts may be able to testify that the firing pin impressions found on the recovered casings are identical to or similar to test fired rounds.

Examination of the victim and the victim's clothing can provide important information concerning the estimated distance the victim was from the suspect when the firearm was discharged. **Stippling** is a pattern of tiny abrasions on the skin that surround the entrance wound and is caused by unburned particles of gunpowder striking the skin. Stippling cannot be washed off. Entrance wounds that have stippling indicate that the firearm was within two feet of the victim's body when the gun was discharged.

FIGURE 8.2: *Circle in center of casing is a firing pin impression*

Tool Marks and Other Impressions

Some tool marks are unique. When an expert analyst compares an impression to a certain tool, he/she can confirm whether that tool left the mark in question. This may require microscopic analysis. Shoe and tire prints can be very important evidence. The direction and number of shoe prints at a scene will help investigators reconstruct the scene and give insight to how many people were present at the event. Photographing and making casts of the prints make it possible for the analyst to compare the prints left at the scene with shoes recovered later in the investigation. Large laboratories have files of shoe patterns that help identify the manufacturer of the shoe associated with a case.

Questioned Documents

Many cases have documents associated with the crime. This is true not only of white-collar crime cases, but also crimes against persons.

Issues associated with questioned documents are:

- Who is the author?

- Is the document a forgery?

- Is the document an original?

- Where did the paper originate?

In addition to identifying who wrote a document, examiners may be able to make inferences about the author's level of education and region of origin. Contrary to statements by some handwriting experts, it is not always possible to definitively conclude that a suspect wrote a specific document. However, in cases where the document examiner is able to identify the writer of a document, the results are an effective tool for the investigator.

CASE STUDY

A suspect committed an armed robbery of a Burger King restaurant. The suspect handed the manager of the restaurant a note, which told the manager to be calm and do what he was told. When the suspect was arrested a couple of days later, driving the manager's car, the suspect told police that he purchased the vehicle from two men. Inside the vehicle were several notes that had the same wording used in the Burger King robbery. The car also contained a diary, listing the "surveillance" that the suspect did of various fast-food restaurants in the area. The suspect contended that the diary belonged to the men who sold him the car.

Using handwriting analysis, what steps can be taken to connect the suspect to the documents and to the robbery?

DNA

DNA evidence is probably the single most significant and trusted evidence in the history of forensics. It is also the most likely evidence to be left at, or taken from, a scene. In part, that is because everyone has DNA, which can be obtained from blood, saliva, or sweat, but also because microscopic samples of DNA could be left at a scene without the suspect's knowledge.

Forensic serologists concentrate on the chromosomal regions that differ from individual to individual, and identify a unique DNA profile for a person. Once this profile is identified, it can be compared to unknown DNA profiles found at the scene of a crime, or on other pieces of evidence, to determine if they match. Prior to DNA profiling, serologists relied on blood grouping, which was nearly as definitive.

DNA evidence can not only be used to identify and convict the guilty, it can be used to exonerate the wrongly convicted. While DNA evidence is considered to be the biggest advance in forensic science, it isn't the definitive answer in all cases. DNA evidence found at a scene may be very significant; it may also be relatively insignificant. Finding a suspect's DNA on his murdered wife does not prove that he killed her. We are constantly picking up DNA profiles from people we come in contact with. If a suspect denies having been around the victim and the suspect's DNA is subsequently found on the victim, the significance of that information is very high. However, finding a DNA profile doesn't relieve the investigator of doing a thorough investigation. DNA evidence doesn't resolve the issue of consent in sexual assault cases. It doesn't resolve the issue of affirmative defenses such as self-defense or intoxication, and it doesn't give investigators the identity of a shooter if two suspects were at the scene. It doesn't give a specific time as to when the DNA profile was deposited. Most importantly, recovered DNA has no value unless there is another matching DNA profile. In some cases, there may be some DNA related material, but the material is of such a small quantity that a profile cannot be established.

Summary

Forensics plays a major role in modern investigations. Some members of the general public have a misperception of what forensics can and cannot provide with regard to an investigation. Additionally, forensics is not uniformly available to all agencies. It is not uncommon for major city departments to have their own forensic labs, but the remainder of the state may have only one lab that has to continually evaluate and determine the priority of what is to be tested. Unlike television, real forensic labs cannot test everything, and they don't always come up with definitive answers that lead to the conviction of the suspect, even if he or she is guilty.

A working knowledge of forensic science is of great benefit to any investigator. While non-law enforcement investigators may not be held to the same standard as their law enforcement counterparts concerning the chain of evidence, every investigator must do everything possible to maintain the integrity of any seized evidence.

As technology grows, so will advances in the field of forensic science. Thanks to these advances, physical evidence can help establish what happened during the commission of a crime. As these sciences become more advanced, there will be less reliance on victim or witness statements and testimony. However, forensics will never completely replace good investigative techniques; rather forensics will supplement those techniques.

Discussion Questions

1. Discuss how forensic science can make a case stronger.

2. Explain how trace evidence can make a case stronger, even if the recovered trace evidence is determined to have only class characteristics.

3. Discuss the type of forensic evidence you would expect to find in a white-collar crime investigation

4. Discuss how you, as the lead investigator on a sexual assault case that occurred in a wooded area, would avoid destroying or compromising evidence.

5. Discuss the issues associated with the five stages related to forensic evidence.

Exercises

1. Pick a type of forensic evidence, i.e. DNA, fingerprints, ballistics. What does this type of evidence provide? What are the downsides of this type of evidence? How do you preserve this type of evidence? How is the evidence admitted into court?

2. Pick a forensic specialty, such as Forensic Pathology or Forensic Anthropology. Describe what the specialty is and what it can provide to an investigation. What qualifications does the specialty require?

3. Watch an episode of your favorite crime show. What types of trace evidence were associated with the crime committed in the episode? Did you think of some types of trace evidence associated with the crime that the episode didn't cover?

4. Assume the following factors exist in a crime you are investigating: A man is found shot in his bedroom. Investigators recovered a gun, two spent bullets, a partially smoked cigarette, and a cup with lipstick on it. Write the chain-of-custody for each of these items from the time they are seized until they are presented in court. (Hint: Various types of testing and/or analysis are associated with these items.)

Resources

Exhibit E

SAMPLE FORM
PROPERTY SIGN-OUT SHEET
EXHIBIT E

Case Number: _____   Evidence Tag Number: _____

Item Number	Description of Property (one item only)						
Date/Time Out	Property Received by (name#)	Signature	Property Released by (name#)	Destination Court, DA, Lab	Property Returned by (name#)	Date/Time Returned	Property Officer Signature

The Property Sign-Out sheet is a secondary form that can be used to track property/evidence that has been signed out for court, etc.

Having the proper documentation on the original Evidence Report/Property Tag form (Exhibit E in Module 5), is always preferred. This form provides a tool to easily audit property that hasn't been returned.

Key Terms

Algor Mortis: the process by which the body decreases to the room temperature after death.

Arches/Loops/Whorls: characteristics associated with an individual's fingerprints.

Autopsy: a postmortem examination of a body to determine cause and manner of death.

Ballistics: the analysis of bullets and bullet impacts.

Class Characteristics: the evidence being compared has measurable features in common, but it cannot be determined whether the items came from the same source.

Cranial Examination: the examination of the brain during an autopsy.

CSI Syndrome: the public perception that forensic science plays a major role in criminal trials.

Defensive Wounds: injuries found on a victim and associated with the victim trying to defend or shield themselves.

Firing Pin: that part of firearm that strikes the live round.

Forensic Science: the application of various sciences to answer questions associated with the legal system.

Gross Examination: refers to the external examination of a deceased during an autopsy.

Gunshot Residue: the particles that are expelled from a firearm when the firearm is fired.

Individual Characteristics: one piece of evidence is measurably certain to have come from the same source as the piece of evidence with which it is being compared.

Integrated Automated Fingerprint Identification System (IAFIS): an FBI database maintained for the search and comparison of fingerprints.

Livor Mortis: the process following death in which the blood begins to settle in parts of the body that are closest to the ground due to gravitational, causing reddish or dark areas on the skin. Also known as lividity, livor mortis can help establish a time frame of death.

Rigor Mortis: the process by which various muscles stiffen after death.

Striations: the marks left on a fired bullet as it leaves the barrel.

Stippling: the pattern of tiny abrasions to the skin that surround the entrance of a gunshot wound.

Toxicology: the stage of an autopsy where levels of substances, such as drugs or poisons, are measured.

Trace Evidence: evidence that is taken or left at the scene.

Transfer Evidence: a type of trace evidence that is transferred from one source to another.

Weight: a legal term referring to the amount of significance a piece of evidence has in court.

MODULE 9
Legal Concepts

Key Module Concepts:

- The role of standing as it relates to consent searches

- The differences between a custodial stop and an arrest

- The requirements relating to when an individual must be read the Miranda Warning

- Exceptions to the search warrant requirement of the Fourth Amendment

Introduction

A police detective entered the interview room and sat across from a suspect in a series of armed robberies in the metropolitan area. Before the detective could say anything, the suspect told the detective, "I did it." The detective advised the suspect of his Miranda Rights, but did not obtain a waiver of rights from the suspect. The suspect went on to tell the detective that all of the stolen items were at a hiding place in the mountains. The suspect offered to take the detective there. At the hiding place, detectives found a large number of items that were reported stolen over the past two years. During the suppression hearing, the court ruled that the suspect's statements and the recovered property are inadmissible at trial because the suspect did not waive his Miranda Rights.

Similar scenarios occur every day within law enforcement agencies throughout the country. What occurred, how it occurred, and how it is presented to the court will determine whether the recovered items and the defendant's statement are admissible in court. If the court rules that the statements or the seized items are **suppressed**, meaning that the seized items and/or statement cannot be introduced into evidence against the defendant, there may not be a prosecutable case. It is critical that investigators have a good, working knowledge of search and seizure, Miranda Warnings, and other Constitutional issues. Otherwise there is a strong possibility that items seized during an investigation or a defendant's statements may be inadmissible in court. If evidence is not admitted, the criminal case may be greatly compromised, resulting in an acquittal or dismissal of charges.

Ask Yourself

- *Why are government searches and seizures so regulated?*
- *What are the sanctions for violating the Fourth Amendment?The Fourth Amendment*
- *The Fourth Amendment to the United States Constitution reads as follows:*

Example

"The right of the people to be secure in their persons, houses, papers, and effects, against unreasonable searches and seizures, shall not be violated, and no Warrants shall issue, but upon probable cause, supported by Oath or affirmation, and particularly describing the place to be searched, and the persons or things to be seized."

This single paragraph provides the framework for courts in determining whether **governmental actions** were proper regarding the search and seizure of evidence. If the court determines that the government agents (law enforcement) acted properly, the seized items will be admitted into evidence during the trial. If the court determines that the government action was improper, the items will not be introduced into evidence. The Fourth Amendment does not apply to actions of private citizens who conduct searches and seize evidence, unless the private citizen was acting as an agent of law enforcement. When employing an **agent of law enforcement,** a citizen is retained by law enforcement to do something that would require the agency to comply with Fourth Amendment requirements.

Example

Example A:
A law enforcement investigator enters a residence and seizes items from inside the residence. The court will evaluate the investigator's actions to determine whether the seized items will be admitted as evidence in any criminal proceeding.

Example B:
A private citizen entered a residence and seized items from inside the residence. The citizen then turned the items over to law enforcement. If law enforcement asked the citizen to go into the residence and seize the items when law enforcement would have needed a warrant, the court would find that the citizen was an agent of law enforcement and suppress the seized items. If the citizen acted on his or her own and turned the seized items over to law enforcement, the seized items would be admitted as evidence.

Citizens have an expectation of privacy from unreasonable searches and seizures. The privacy aspect must be legitimate, meaning that the expectation of privacy is one that society readily acknowledges. Citizens have a legitimate expectation of privacy of their homes, but there is no legitimate expectation of privacy in areas that are open to the public.

Search and Seizure

What constitutes a search and seizure? A **search** occurs when an officer/investigator uses one of his five senses to "look" into an area. A **seizure** occurs when something is actually taken.

Example

An investigator walks into a room and smells marijuana. He looks around the room and sees a baggie sitting on the table. (This would constitute a search.) The investigator then picks up the baggie, because he knows it is illegal for a person to possess marijuana. This would constitute a seizure.

Warrants

A **warrant** is a legal document that authorizes a law enforcement officer to take action. In the case of an **arrest warrant**, the document authorizes law enforcement officers to arrest a specific person for a specific crime. In the case of a **search warrant**, the document authorizes law enforcement officers to search a specific location for specific evidence of a crime.

Warrants are comprised of two sections: the warrant itself, which provides information concerning

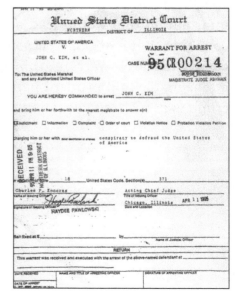

FIGURE 9.1: *Warrants are legal documents that are a required step in the judicial process.*

who is to be arrested or the area to be searched, and an **affidavit**, in which the law enforcement officer obtaining the warrant gives an oath that the information contained in the affidavit is correct. Once the judge approves the warrant and affidavit, the judge signs the warrant and puts his official seal on it. The affidavit is a narrative of the investigative information that establishes probable cause for the search warrant or the arrest warrant. Warrants must be presented to a **neutral magistrate**, meaning that the judge reviewing the warrant/affidavit does not have any involvement or association with the case for which the warrant is being sought.

As discussed in Module One, probable cause is the standard law enforcement officers must meet to either arrest a person or obtain a search warrant. In the case of an arrest warrant, probable cause would be the information obtained during the course of the investigation that establishes that the suspect committed a specific crime. For a search warrant, probable cause would be the information obtained during the course of an investigation that establishes that evidence associated with the alleged crime is in a specific location. In legal terms, probable cause is defined as that information that would lead a reasonable and prudent person to conclude that a specific person committed a specific crime; in the case of a search warrant, this would be information that would lead a reasonable and prudent person to conclude that evidence of a crime is at a specific location.

Example

Example A: Probable Cause for an Arrest Warrant
Joseph Watkins entered a gas station and robbed the clerk. As Watkins was leaving the store, a patrol car pulled up to the gas station and ordered Watkins to stop. When the officer stopped Watkins, the clerk came out of the store and told the officer that Watkins had just robbed the clerk. When the officer searched Watkins, the officer found a gun and a wad of money in Watkins' left front pants pocket. The officer also obtained surveillance video from the store showing Watkins committing the robbery. Here, probable cause was established that Watkins committed the crime of robbery.

Example B: Probable Cause for a Search Warrant
Anthony Perry and Gary Simmons attended a party, during which a fight broke out. Mr. Perry pulled a gun and shot one of the other guests. Mr. Perry and Mr. Simmons left the party and drove to Mr. Perry's house, where Mr. Perry put the gun in a dresser drawer. The next day, investigators interviewed Mr. Perry and Mr. Simmons because another guest had gotten Mr. Perry's license plate number when he left the scene of the shooting. Mr. Simmons told investigators that Mr. Perry had the gun in the dresser drawer.

Police obtained a search warrant for the gun in the dresser. In this situation, probable cause was established that the gun used in the shooting was in the dresser drawer.

Other Considerations Associated with Warrants

Standing

The legal term "standing" means that the person has a possessory or proprietary interest in the property being searched. If the defendant can't show that his Constitutional rights were violated, the evidence will be admitted.

Example

Example A:

A police officer asks the owner of a house if the officer can search the owner's house. During the search, items belonging to the defendant were seized. The defendant cannot contest the seizing of the items because the defendant does not have standing to contest the seizure of items in someone else's house.

Example B:

A police officer asks the defendant's neighbor for consent to search the defendant's house. If the neighbor doesn't have any proprietary interest in the defendant's house, the search will be deemed to be unlawful and the evidence will be suppressed.

Reliability of Information

Reliability, or veracity, of information refers to the the information contained within the affidavit. Some sources of information are automatically considered reliable, such as witnesses, law enforcement officers, and forensic pathologists. Reliability in those situations requires nothing more than the name and date of birth (for lay witnesses), or their name and title.

Example

- On January 24, 2011, Englewood Police Officer Jason Kimball responded to the residence located at 1378 West Jackson Street.
- Wilma Carter (date of birth: 05/24/1986), who lived next door to the victim, told investigators ...
- Dr. Ben Gates, a forensic pathologist, performed the autopsy on the victim.

In cases involving informants, the courts require a showing that the informant provided reliable information in the past, that the the informant's information was corroborated, or some other means of showing the informant's credibility.

Stale Information

The information contained in a search warrant affidavit must be current. Information is considered stale if it is unlikely that the item(s) to be seized are still present at the place to be searched.

Example

Warren Thompson committed a residential burglary two months ago during which he stole a television and a laptop computer. Most burglars get rid of stolen items by either fencing or pawning them as soon as possible. Unless there is information that Mr. Thompson currently has the items in his residence, the likelihood that the stolen items are still in Mr. Thompson's residence is remote; as such, this is considered stale information.

Good Faith

The courts have held that law enforcement officers may make mistakes as long as the mistakes are reasonable. If a law enforcement officer/investigator acts in **good faith**, evidence may be admitted in court even if the evidence was collected in violation of the Fourth Amendment. In determining whether the officer/investigator was acting in good faith, the court can take into consideration the officer's actions, experience, and knowledge. The prosecution must assert the "good faith" exception.

Example

Officers served a search warrant on a residence and it was later determined that the warrant was defective in some manner. The court may determine that although the warrant was defective, the investigator was acting in good faith, and the evidence will be admitted.

Execution of Warrants

Contrary to what we see in movies and television, not every search warrant is executed by breaking down doors and charging in with a SWAT team. The execution of the search warrant must be reasonable, meaning that the degree of intrusion must be justified based upon the totality of the circumstances. Executing a search warrant on a drug house where the suspects are known to possess and use weapons, or a residence where a suspected killer is hiding, is significantly different than executing a search warrant on a residence where a computer fraud suspect resides.

In most states, a "knock and announce" is required unless the investigator filing the search warrant affidavit can articulate a basis for a no-knock warrant. A **no-knock warrant** is issued by a judge and allows law enforcement officers to enter a premise without knocking or announcing their presence. The basis for the no-knock warrant is that there is a known risk of serious bodily injury to the officers, or that evidence associated with the crime will be destroyed. If law enforcement officers don't obtain a no-knock warrant and then execute the warrant without announcing, there may be sanctions against the officers.

Authority to Detain Individuals Pending a Search Warrant

Sometimes when investigators execute a search warrant in a residence, there are individuals present. Investigators are authorized to detain or exclude individuals from the residence during the execution of the search warrant.

Exceptions to Warrant Requirement

Other than exceptions that have been established through case law, any search by government agents must be initiated by a search warrant. The Supreme Court has held that whenever practical, law enforcement officers should obtain a warrant. The court will initially assume that all searches conducted without a search warrant are unreasonable. However, courts recognize a number of exceptions to the warrant requirement.

Consent

Consent does not require either reasonable suspicion or probable cause. Investigators can ask anyone at any time for consent to search. The requirements for a valid consent search are that the person has the authority to give consent, that the consent was freely and voluntarily given, and the consent was not a result of any duress or coercion.

Investigators must be sure that the person giving consent has the authority to do so. In determining such authority, investigators must determine the degree of expectation of privacy and who has standing to give consent. This is not always an easy task to determine. Sometimes people share common areas, while other times there is exclusive control of an area, meaning that only one person has access (such as a person who is renting a room in someone's house).

As to the "free and voluntary" aspect, the person giving the consent must be aware that he or she has the authority to either grant or deny consent of a search. If the person is able to show the court that he didn't realized he could deny consent, the fruits of the search will be suppressed.

Coercion and duress may come in many forms. The classic example is of an investigator telling a person that if he doesn't consent to a search, the investigator will get a warrant. In such a situation, the court ruled that the consent was coerced, and thus the items seized are suppressed. If an investigator uses promises or threats to obtain consent, any evidence obtained will be suppressed.

The best practice concerning consent searches is to have the person sign a "consent to search" form, as seen in Exhibit D of Module Three. The form should inform the person that he has the right to refuse consent and that the consent is being given freely and voluntarily.

The courts have also held that the person giving consent can limit the scope of the search, meaning he can tell the investigators where they can and cannot search.

Incident to a Lawful Arrest

Most departments require that officers/investigators conduct a search of an arrested individual. This is done without a warrant. The justification for this exception is that the suspect may access something to escape, cause injury to the officer or others, or destroy evidence. The officer/investigator can search the area "within the immediate control" of the arrestee.

If the person was driving a car at the time of his arrest, the passenger compartment can be searched only for offense-related evidence. If an individual is arrested for a warrant for "Failure to Appear," under the incident to arrest exception, there is no evidence of that crime, and thus the officer is not authorized to search the vehicle.

Although it may appear to be obvious, the arrest must be lawful, meaning that there was probable cause for the arrest. If the arrest is found to be unlawful, any evidence obtained as a result of a search is inadmissible.

Plain View

Officers may seize items under this exception, providing three conditions are present: the officer/investigator is in a place he has a right to be; the observation of the evidence is inadvertent; and there is a nexus to a crime. Inadvertent means that the investigator didn't plan on seeing the item(s). **Nexus** to a crime means that when the investigator observed the item(s), he knew it was either evidence of a crime or contraband.

The officer may use any of his senses to determine that evidence is present.

Example

A detective goes to a residence to contact a witness. The witness lets the detective into the house (fulfills the requirement of being in a place he has a right to be). While inside the residence, the investigator sees methamphetamine and needles (inadvertent in that he wasn't planning on seeing these items). Since the officer knows methamphetamine is an illegal drug, he seizes the evidence.

Vehicles

If an officer develops probable cause during contact with someone in a vehicle, that vehicle can be searched without a warrant. The basis for this exception is that vehicles are mobile and can move by the time investigators get a warrant. An important point to remember is that if a sealed or locked container is found in the vehicle, that item cannot be searched without a warrant. The item can be seized and held until a warrant is obtained.

Abandoned Property

Keep in mind that the Fourth Amendment secures individuals' interest in property in which they have a reasonable expectation of privacy. However, abandoned property can be searched without a warrant because the expectation of privacy is no longer applicable.

Example

A suspect is using his cellular phone to take up-skirt pictures of females in a store. A police officer sees this activity and attempts to contact the suspect. The suspect runs out of the store and throws his phone into a garbage can. The officer may retrieve the phone and look at the contents because the property has been abandoned.

FIGURE 9.2: *There is no legal expectation of privacy pertaining to abandoned property.*

Open Fields

Because an open field is visible to people other than the individual who owns it, there is a diminished expectation of privacy. If an investigator is driving down the road and sees marijuana plants growing in a field, that information can be used to seize the items or be used to obtain a warrant.

Exigent Circumstances

If there is an immediate need to assist individuals who are seriously injured or who may be threatened with serious bodily injury, law enforcement may enter without a warrant. This exception requires an objectively reasonable basis for believing the person in the residence is in imminent danger.

Example

An officer responds to a call of domestic violence. As the officer approaches the residence, he hears loud voices and a woman's scream. It would be unrealistic to expect an officer to have to get a warrant to enter the residence in such instances. The officer may enter the residence and ascertain what the situation is. Once the situation is under control, the officer cannot conduct a thorough search of the house based upon the exigent circumstances exception.

Another form of exigent circumstances is the possibility of destruction of evidence. As with the situation involving potential serious bodily injury, the officer must be able to articulate the basis for the intrusion. Officers and investigators must balance the risk of the intrusion with the type of evidence to be seized. In most states, officers would not be justified in breaking down the door of a residence to secure an individual who was suspected of driving while intoxicated. In situations where the suspect may be flushing drugs down a toilet or getting rid of a weapon, such an intrusion may be warranted.

Inventory Searches

The purpose of an inventory search is to account for items that may be in a vehicle tin a police impound lot. If contraband or evidence of a crime is found during the course of the inventory search, the evidence will be admissible as long as two conditions are met:

- The department has a written policy concerning inventory searches

- Inventory searches are conducted on all vehicles in the impound lot

Dwellings

There are numerous means by which a lawful search of a dwelling may occur:

- Search warrant for that specific residence

- An arrest warrant, if the person named in the search warrant lives at that dwelling

- Exigent circumstances, such as hot pursuit, an emergency situation, or possible destruction of contraband/evidence

- Consent

Officers/investigators can also conduct a limited search of a residence under the protective sweep premise. The key component to a protective sweep is that the officers/investigators can only look in those areas where a threat may be located.

Example

Officers respond to a dispatch call at a residence. When the officers enter the residence, they find a male lying on the floor with two gunshot wounds to his chest. The officers may conduct a search of the residence for suspects or other injured parties, but can only search those areas where other victims and/or suspects may be located. Evidence found in areas such as dressers, medicine cabinets, and desks would be inadmissible under the protective sweep exception. The protective sweep exception does not authorize officers/ investigators to search for evidence.

There is no "homicide exception" to the warrant requirement. The only reason a search may be conducted initially in such situations is for the limited purpose of finding other victims or suspects. Anything that is observed during the search is subject to seizure, but a better practice is to note the location of possible evidence and include it in a search warrant.

Contact with People

If a police officer or investigator approaches a person and starts to talk to him, there is no "seizure" of that person. As such, no justification for the contact is needed. If the person starts to walk away and the investigator impedes the person from moving, then the investigator needs to demonstrate there was at least "reasonable suspicion" to detain the person.

An investigator must meet a standard of "reasonable suspicion" to make an investigatory stop of a person. An **investigatory stop** means that a person is stopped and is not free to leave, at least for a limited time. This limited seizure of a person is to ascertain whether the person is associated with some criminal activity. The stop must be limited in the amount of time the person is detained, as well as the scope of the stop.

Example

A little girl is kidnapped from in front of her residence. The little girl's mother sees the suspect's car drive off. She is able to tell the investigators that it is a black two-door sports car with a white stripe going down the middle of the car. Investigators see a car fitting that description within five blocks of where the little girl was kidnapped. The investigators can stop the vehicle and detain the driver long enough to ascertain if the driver was involved in the kidnapping. If, during the stop, the investigators are unable to develop information indicating that the stopped driver was involved in the kidnapping, the investigators must let the driver go.

An arrest must be based upon probable cause. The initial stop may be based upon reasonable suspicion, with probable cause developing during the course of contact.

The key issue concerning law enforcement's contact with citizens is whether the citizen believed that he was free to leave. Courts look at the totality of circumstances to help determine whether the citizen was restrained, including the following questions:

- Did the investigator exert physical control over the individual?

- How many law enforcement officers were there?

- Did the officers display weapons?

- What was the tone of the officer's voice?

- Did the officer do anything to impede the person's movement?

Although an encounter may initially be consensual, it could progress to either a reasonable suspicion or probable cause situation.

Example

An investigator is driving down a highway when he sees a person hitchhiking on the side of the road. The officer pulls over and gets out of his vehicle. The officer notices that the person has blood on the front of his clothing. The person tells the officer that he is not hurt and that he doesn't know where the blood came from. The officer conducts a pat-down of the person and finds a knife that has blood on it. The officer puts the person in the back of the patrol car and calls for backup. Here, the initial contact was consensual, and as the contact between the officer and the person progressed, the reasonable suspicion threshold was met. However, the officer isn't at the probable cause threshold yet, because he doesn't know where the blood came from. It could be a result of a homicide, or something much less diabolical.

Motor Vehicle

Investigators may search a vehicle:

- With a search warrant

- If the investigator has probable cause

- Incidental to a lawful arrest

- While taking inventory of the vehicle

- With consent

If an officer/investigator stops an individual who is driving a stolen vehicle, the driver doesn't have any standing to object to a search of the vehicle. Anything found in the vehicle during such a search can be used against the driver or the owner of the vehicle. If an owner gives someone permission to drive their vehicle, the driver has standing to object to any search of the vehicle.

Violations of Constitutional Rights

What happens when a Constitutional violation occurs? Usually the allegation of a Constitutional violation occurs during a **motions hearing**. As part of the motions hearing, defense counsel may argue that evidence seized during the investigation was obtained in violation of the defendant's Constitutional rights. If the judge rules in favor of the defense, the **exclusionary rule** comes into play. Under the exclusionary rule, any evidence that was illegally obtained, i.e. in violation of the defendant's Constitutional rights, is excluded. Such violations may also result in:

- **Injunctions**: a court order that orders parties to do or refrain from doing a certain act

- **Declaratory judgments**: the judgment in a civil case that is legally binding to the parties involved

- **Damages**: part of the award given in a civil case

If a court rules that evidence is suppressed, any evidence seized as a result of that illegal seizure is also excluded. This is known as **Fruit of the Poisonous Tree**. If the investigator is able to establish with the court that the evidence would have been obtained under the concept of inevitable discovery, the evidence may be admitted. Under the **inevitable discovery theory**, the prosecution would argue that the evidence would have eventually been found by law enforcement by other means.

Example

A suspect gives a statement to law enforcement officers, which leads the officers to the grave site of the victim. If the court throws out the defendant's statement, the prosecution may still be able to get in the information concerning the grave site if the prosecutor can show that investigators would have found the grave site independent of the information obtained in the defendant's statement.

CASE STUDY

Two individuals are accused of the execution-style deaths of a teenage male and his girlfriend. Information obtained during the course of the investigation included the following:

- The victims were known associates of the suspects, purchasing and selling drugs on their behalf

- A known associate of the suspects told investigators that the suspects wanted to kill the male teenager because the suspects believed he "snitched" on the suspects concerning an earlier shooting

- The known associate also told investigators that a female teenager accompanied the suspects when the shootings occurred and that the guns used in the shooting were at the female teenager's residence

- The known associate also told investigators that the victims were transported to a field in the trunk of the vehicle belonging to one of the suspects

- The victims were found gagged with duct tape and covered with hoodies, which the parents of the victims stated they did not belong to their children

- The male victim was barefoot when he was found. His parents told investigators that he had been wearing expensive basketball shoes when he was last seen.

- The parents of the male victim also told investigators that he had a wallet and routinely carried cash on him at all times. Investigators did not find the victim's wallet.

- The investigation established that the victims were not shot at the location where their bodies were recovered

- When one of the suspects was arrested on a previous case and incarcerated, he told a fellow inmate that he and the other suspect had killed two teenagers for being "snitches"

Is there enough information to obtain search warrants? If not, what additional information would you need? What would you obtain search warrants for? What evidence are you hoping to locate? What exceptions to the search warrant requirement could be used?

Miranda Warnings

In 1966, the United States Supreme Court rendered an opinion in *Miranda v. Arizona,* a case that would forever change the way suspects in custody are interviewed. When law enforcement officers have a suspect in custody and intend to interrogate, the suspect must be given with what has become known as the Miranda Warning.

The definition of custody, as it relates to the Miranda Warning, continues to be refined. Generally, **custody** is defined as being under arrest or otherwise deprived of freedom of movement in any significant way. If the person had been placed in handcuffs, transported to a police station or sheriff's office, and placed in a cell, there is no question that the individual is in custody. But what about the situation where the individual is contacted at the scene and the investigators determine that they don't have enough information to arrest the suspect, but want to talk to him at the police station? Many departments require that individuals who are placed in the backseat of a police car must be handcuffed for safety reasons. Does that constitute an arrest?

It is common for investigators to ask potential suspects to come to the police station for an interview. In such a situation, a person could argue that his freedom of movement is significantly inhibited. Since the Miranda decision, the courts have continually refined what constitutes "custody" by reviewing the totality of the circumstances. If an individual meets officers in a police station and it is made very clear that the individual is free to leave at any time, and that when either the individual asks to leave or the investigators conclude the interview, the individual leaves the station, there is not an in-custody situation.

On the other hand, if the investigator tells the individual that he is not under arrest, but the individual is not allowed to leave, can't make calls, and is formally arrested after the interview, the courts have found that the individual was in custody.

Here are some factors that the court takes into consideration when looking at the totality of the circumstances to determine if the individual was in custody:

- How was the individual transported to the police station? Was he allowed to drive his own vehicle or have someone drive him, or was he transported in a police vehicle?

- How many law enforcement officers initially contacted the individual?

- Were the officers armed? At any time during the initial contact did any officer pull his gun or use any force in having the individual comply?

- Was the individual allowed to contact friends, relatives, or another party? Were there any restrictions on contact?

- At the police station, how many investigators were involved in the interview? Were the investigators' guns and handcuffs visible during the interview?

- In the interview room, were the investigators sitting between the individual and the door of the interview room? Was the interview room door open or closed? If the door was closed, did the investigators explain why the door was closed?

- Did the individual ever ask to leave the room or terminate the interview, or was he told that he couldn't terminate the interview?

- At the conclusion of the interview, was the individual arrested or allowed to leave?

The interrogation component of Miranda has also been a topic of court interpretations. In essence, any time an investigator is attempting to get a person to confess to something, it is defined as an interrogation. Since the definition of "interview" and "interrogation" are often interchangeable, it is best to consider any conversation with potential suspects as an interrogation.

Miranda held that both components (in custody and interrogation) must be present for Miranda to apply. If only one of the components exists, the Miranda Warning need not be given.

Example

Example A:

An investigator contacts a potential suspect in a case at the suspect's house. Although the interview may be considered an "interrogation," the suspect is being contacted at his home and at the conclusion of the interview/interrogation, the investigator leaves and the suspect remains at his home. No Miranda Warnings are required.

Example B:

A suspect is arrested at the scene of the crime and placed in the back seat of a patrol car. While on the way to the police station, the suspect starts telling the officer what happened. If it can be established that the officer did not ask the suspect any questions or further the conversation, all of the suspect's statements would be admissible, although no Miranda Warning was given.

FIGURE 9.3: *Suspects in custody must be read the Miranda Warning.*

Giving Miranda Warnings

If the investigator determines that a Miranda Warning is to be given, the procedure is comprised of two components:

- Having the individual understand his rights under Miranda

- Having the individual waive his Miranda Rights

Although many investigators have memorized the Miranda Warning, it is recommended that the investigator use a Miranda Rights form. The form contains the Miranda Rights, a section for the individual being interviewed to sign noting that he understands his Rights, and a section for the individual to sign indicating that he is waiving his Miranda Rights and is willing to talk to the investigator. See Exhibit G in the Resources section for a sample form.

Before stating the Miranda Warning, the investigator should ask the individual if he is on any medication, under the influence of alcohol or drugs, and should confirm that no promises or threats have been made to the individual.

It is recommended that the investigator read each section of the Miranda Warning and have the individual acknowledge that he understands. Many investigators have the individual place his initials beside each section as it is read.

After reading the Miranda Rights, the individual should sign the section of the Miranda form dealing with the understanding of the Miranda Rights.

The investigator should then read the waiver portion of the Miranda form, have the individual read and sign the waiver section, if the individual is willing to talk to the investigator.

Once the Miranda Rights form is completed, and the individual has waived his rights, the investigator may start the interview. If at any time the individual indicates in any manner that he wishes to consult with an attorney, the interview must be terminated. Although an individual may answer some questions or volunteer information, the individual is not deprived of the right to refrain from answering some questions or terminate the interview.

Issues Associated With Miranda Warnings

Knowing Waiver

Sometimes there is an educational or language barrier between investigator and interviewee. In the case of an educational barrier, the investigator must make sure the individual understands what his rights are, and what it means to waive those rights. By the same token, the investigator must be careful not to use wording that changes the meaning of the Miranda Rights. The use of a "knowing waiver" to ensure that the individual is aware of his/her rights and the ramifications of waiving those rights is required.

If a language barrier exists, investigators should call on a translator to ensure that the individual understands the Miranda Rights and can provide a valid waiver.

Juveniles

In some states, a juvenile who is a potential suspect must have a parent or legal guardian present before any questioning. This is true even in cases where the juvenile wants to talk to the investigator. If someone other than the parent is present, the court will require that the investigator show that reasonable steps were taken to ensure that the party representing himself as a guardian is truly a guardian for the child.

Unclear Declarations by the Interviewee

Sometimes the interviewee may say something that isn't a clear indication that the individual wants to terminate the interview or talk to an attorney. The investigator has to make a decision whether the individual's statement is a request to terminate the interview or not. If the investigator continues the interview, but the court determines the statement to be a request to terminate the interview, anything the individual says from that point on will be suppressed.

Example

During the course of an interview, the suspect asks the investigator if she should get a lawyer. The investigator should read the Miranda Warnings again to the suspect, and ask if she wants to continue the interview. If the suspect asks the interviewer the same question a little later in the interview, some courts may find that the second question constitutes a request for an attorney.

Potential Duress Situations

Even though the individual may agree to be interviewed, the investigator needs to be aware of potential duress factors that may render part or all of the statement inadmissible. Being deprived of food, water, or access to a bathroom are such factors. The length and location of the interview can also come into play.

Sometimes the interview is conducted right after a devastating and emotion-evoking event. The court will take such factors into consideration when determining the voluntary status of the statement.

The number of investigators involved in the interview, the investigators' demeanor during the course of the interview, and threatening to charge the individual with as many counts as possible are also potential duress factors.

Potential Promises

Perceived promises on the part of the investigator may also render part or all of the statement inadmissible. If an investigator guarantees that the suspect will be placed in a certain section of the detention facility in exchange for the truth, or offers the suspect food as a condition of talking, the court may well determine that the investigator was making a promise to the suspect in exchange for information.

If the investigator tells the individual that the investigator will talk to the District Attorney handling the case and have the individual charged with a lesser crime, the courts again may see that as a promise.

Example

The defendant was arrested in a mall shooting where one person died. While in custody, police began an interrogation that lasted about three hours. At the beginning of the interrogation, the defendant was provided a written copy of the Miranda Warning. An officer read the defendant his rights and asked the defendant to sign the form to demonstrate that he understood those rights. At no point did the defendant say he wanted to remain silent, that he did not want to talk to the police, or that he wanted an attorney. He was mostly silent during the interrogation, although he gave a few limited verbal responses or nodded his head. Toward the end of the interrogation, the defendant was asked whether he prayed "to God to forgive you for shooting that boy down," to which the defendant responded, "Yes." The court held that the defendant "impliedly waived his Miranda Rights." (Berghuis v. Thompkins)

Summary

This module provided an overview of the warrant requirements as set forth in the Fourth Amendment, some of the court-recognized exceptions to the warrant situation, and the Miranda Warning. Search and seizure issues are relevant to criminal law, and the courts are constantly addressing these issues. Although the United States Supreme Court decisions apply to all states, individual state courts have rendered opinions on these topics that may be more restrictive than the U.S. Supreme Court decisions.

Investigators require a strong working knowledge of search and seizure issues. Failure to understand the court decisions associated with search and seizure can result in the suppression of key pieces of evidence, or sanctions by the court. If investigators work months on a case and then have evidence suppressed, it is devastating to the case, to the investigator, and most importantly to the victims and their families. Sometimes the suppression of evidence leads to a dismissal of a case.

The Fourth Amendment applies to government actions, i.e. law enforcement actions. A corporate investigator or a private investigator is not bound by the same standards addressed in this Module. If a private investigator unlawfully enters a residence or unlawfully obtains potential evidence, the evidence may still be submitted to the court. However, the private investigator may face potential criminal charges for his action, such as trespassing or burglary for the unlawful entry into the residence.

A two-pronged situation must exist before the Miranda Warning is required: custody and interrogation. If either of these components is missing, Miranda does not apply. Ensuring that a suspect's statements are admitted at trial doesn't end with a valid Miranda Warning. The investigator must ensure that the waiver was given knowingly and voluntarily, that the statement was not obtained under duress, and that no promises were made to the suspect in exchange for information during the course of the interrogation.

While some of these requirements may seem restrictive, the premise is to protect an individual's privacy from arbitrary government intrusion. Understanding these Constitutional issues not only help investigators put together cases that the court will accept, but help protect the privacy of individuals.

Discussion Questions

1. There is a constant attempt to balance individual rights with public order. Do you think court decisions provide a balance between an individual's right to privacy and law enforcement's need to act for the public good? Should the courts be more or less restrictive of law enforcement's actions?

2. If there is a violation of a person's Miranda Rights, should the court throw out the statement, or should the officer be sanctioned and the statement allowed in?

3. Should the exceptions to the warrant requirement cited in the text be more or less restrictive?

4. Should the good faith exception be a basis for allowing evidence to be admitted?

5. Discuss how an officer's stop of a person can progress from "reasonable suspicion" to "probable cause."

Exercises

1. Find the criminal statute for "theft" in your state. What must a local investigator establish to have probable cause to arrest a person for theft?

2. Break into groups and discuss who has standing to object to the admissibility of evidence in the following situations:

   a. Drugs found in a student's locker at a public school
   b. A defendant contends that a co-defendant's statement was obtained in violation of the co-defendant's Constitutional rights
   c. A wife gives consent for police officers to search her husband's tool box in the garage. The wife said she doesn't know what is in the tool box because she has never been in it.

3. Pick one of the recognized exceptions to the warrant requirement. Describe what that exception is and why it is a recognized exception to the warrant requirement. Find a recent case decision that illustrates the exception. (Example: Terry vs. Ohio is the landmark case concerning "stop and frisk.") Describe what the case facts were, as well as the court's ruling.

4. A suspect must be in custody, under interrogation, before a Miranda Warning is required. How can an investigator avoid the "in-custody" aspect if he doesn't want to have a Miranda situation?

Resources

Exhibit F

SAMPLE FORM
MIRANDA WARNING
EXHIBIT F

---

1. **YOU HAVE THE RIGHT TO REMAIN SILENT.**
2. Anything you say can and will be used against you in a court of law.
3. You have the right to talk to a lawyer and have him present with you while you are being questioned.
4. If you cannot afford to hire a lawyer, one will be appointed to represent you before any questioning if you wish.
5. You can decide at any time to exercise these rights and not answer any questions or make any statements.

WAIVER

Do you understand each of these rights I have explained them to you?

Having these rights in mind, do you wish to talk to us now?

☐ I acknowledge I am waiving my rights.

Name: _____   Signature: _____

Officer: _____   Badge Number: _____

Date: _____   Time: _____

Key Terms

Affidavit: the narrative portion of a warrant setting forth the probable cause for the warrant.

Agent of Law Enforcement: a private citizen is retained by law enforcement to do something that would require law enforcement to comply with Fourth Amendment requirements.

Arrest Warrant: the document authorizing law enforcement officers to arrest a specific person for a specific offense. The arrest warrant must be based on probable cause and signed by a judge prior to being executed.

Constitutional Issues: issues that are potential violations of the United States Constitution.

Custody: under arrest or otherwise deprived of freedom of movement in any significant way.

Damages: part of the award given in a civil case.

Declaratory Judgments: the judgment in a civil case that is legally binding to the parties involved.

Exclusionary Rule: doctrine stating that evidence collected in a manner that violates a suspect or defendant's Constitutional rights may be rendered inadmissible at trial.

Fruit of the Poisonous Tree: a legal metaphor that describes illegally obtained evidence.

Good Faith: in criminal law, good faith means that the officer's intentions were good. If the court finds that the officer acted in good faith, the evidence may be admitted.

Governmental Action: refers to that action taken by law enforcement officers.

Inevitable Discovery: a legal doctrine that allows evidence that would otherwise be suppressed at trial due to the exclusionary rule.

Injunctions: a court order that orders parties to do or refrain from doing a certain act.

Investigatory Stop: a person is stopped and is not free to leave, at least for a limited time. This limited seizure of a person is to ascertain whether the person is associated with some criminal activity.

Miranda Warning: information that must be given to all suspects that are in custody and being interrogated; informs the suspect that he has a right to remain silent and to retain counsel before being interviewed.

Motions Hearing: part of the criminal courts process, in which the prosecution and defense request that the court rule on the admissibility or inadmissibility of certain evidence.

Neutral Magistrate: a judge who does not have any involvement or association with the case for which a warrant is being sought.

Nexus: an investigator observes an item knows to be evidence of a crime or contraband.

No-Knock Warrant: a warrant that allows law enforcement officers to enter a property, including a residence, without prior notification (such as ringing a doorbell).

Privacy: the main consideration behind the Fourth Amendment and part of the standard for determining if a search is valid.

Protective Sweep: a non-warrant action by law enforcement for the sole purpose of making sure there is no threat in the area being searched.

Search: use of the five senses to "look" into an area.

Search Warrants: the document authorizing law enforcement to search a specific location and seize specified items. A neutral magistrate must sign the warrant before it can be executed.

Seizure: the act of taking something.

Stale: applies to the likelihood that items to be seized will no longer be in a given location, or that informaiton is no longer relevant.

Standing: an individual's proprietary interest in something; a determining factor in situations involving consent.

Suppressed: cannot be used during the trial.

MODULE 10

Standards of Proof, Courtroom Procedures, and Testimony

Key Module Concepts:

- Procedures associated with criminal and civil actions

- List the various people who play a part in a criminal trial

- The courtroom process in civil and criminal cases

- Prosecutorial discretion and prosecutorial misconduct

- Steps investigators take when preparing to testify

Introduction

Once an investigation is completed, a case may go in several directions. The investigative results may be used in a civil trial; in administrative hearings in which a person is sanctioned for their actions; or in a criminal trial. In criminal cases, the complete investigation is submitted to a District Attorney's Office for filing or presentation to a grand jury. In civil cases, the plaintiff files a complaint against the defendant. The judicial stage affords defendants, in both criminal and civil cases, the opportunity to have their say.

In this module, we will discuss the basic components of both the civil and criminal judicial process. We will discuss the roles of the D.A., defense attorneys, judges, and juries, as well as the various standards that apply at the various stages of the process.

Ask Yourself

- *What goes on during a criminal trial?*
- *Is all of the information concerning a case presented during a trial?*
- *What are the different phases of a criminal court case?*

The Judicial System

Adversarial System

The American court system is an **adversarial system**, meaning that there are two opposing sides and the impartial **trier of the facts** (sometimes referred to as the fact-finders). The trier of the facts, also called the trier of the case, may be a judge or a jury. In most jurisdictions, the defendant has the option of having the case heard by a judge or a jury. The prosecution does not have the option of choosing who will hear the case. This applies to both criminal and civil cases. In criminal cases, the prosecutor represents the state and defense counsel represents the defendant. In civil cases, the party being sued is still referred to as the defendant, but the party bringing the suit is referred to as the **plaintiff**. In the adversarial system, both parties are allowed the opportunity to present their case, following the rules of procedures and rules of evidence. Once the evidence has been presented, the trier of the case makes a decision.

Civil vs. Criminal Law

Even with their commonalities, there are several differences between civil and criminal proceedings. Civil law deals with torts (a civil wrong) such as negligence, libel, contract disputes and accidents. Most often, the plaintiff files a case in an attempt to receive monetary compensation for some act or failure to act. If the plaintiff prevails, compensation may be in the form of actual damages or punitive damages. **Actual damages** are to compensate for actual expenses or losses. **Punitive damages** are awarded when the jury concludes that the defendant should be "punished." The burden of proof in a civil case is preponderance of evidence, as mentioned in Module One, which means the trier of the case must believe, by a margin of 51% or more, that the plaintiff's assertion is true and that he/she is entitled to the relief being sought.

Example

The plaintiff hired the defendant to construct an addition to the plaintiff's house. The defendant took money from the plaintiff, but did not do any work. If a jury decided in favor of the plaintiff, an actual damages verdict means that the defendant would owe the plaintiff the money that the defendant took to construct the add-on. If punitive damages were awarded, the jury could "punish" the defendant by making him pay more money back than was originally taken by the defendant.

State criminal cases deal with alleged violations of statutes enacted by the state legislature. Unlike civil cases, where the remedy is monetary, criminal cases can result in either a fine and/or incarceration. In criminal cases, the action is brought against the defendant by the State. The burden of proof is "beyond a reasonable doubt," which, as noted in Module One, is much greater than the standard found in civil cases. Unlike civil cases, defendants in criminal cases may be arrested and held in jail or requested to post bond, depending on the nature of the case.

Investigators work in both the civil and criminal law realms. While the rules of evidence and other procedures may vary between criminal and civil cases, from an investigator's perspective, they both require the ability to gather facts, conduct effective interviews, and get a complete picture of what occurred.

The Courtroom

The participants in the courtroom include the following individuals:

- The Defendant: the individual who is charged with violating one or more criminal or civil statutes that fall within the jurisdiction of the court

- The Judge: presides over the courtroom proceedings and makes rulings as to what is admissible during the trial. The judge also rules on objections made by attorneys during witness testimony, and sentences the defendant if he is found guilty.

- The Prosecutor/Plaintiff's Attorney: represents the state in criminal cases. Often the prosecutor's office handles district court cases (felony cases) and county court (misdemeanors). City and Municipal Court cases are handled by the city attorney's office. In civil cases, the litigator represents the plaintiff.

- Defense Counsel: represents the defendant. In criminal cases, defense counsel may be privately retained, meaning that the defendant pays for the attorney or may be appointed and paid for by the state. In civil cases, the defendant retains his/her own attorney.

- The Jury: unless the defendant wants his case heard by the court, meaning that the judge will determine guilt or innocence, a jury is the trier of the facts

- Witnesses: the people who testify during the case. As mentioned in previous Modules, witnesses can be lay witnesses or expert witnesses. Investigators testify in court as lay witnesses.

- The Bailiff: is an employee of the court and his primary responsibility is to keep order in the court. Many jurisdictions now have Sheriff's Department Deputies assigned to courtroom security. The deputies are responsible for the transport of defendants who are currently incarcerated.

- The Reporter: the individual who records all of the trial proceedings

- The Clerk: an employee of the court who helps keep the courtroom moving and handles requests from the judge

FIGURE 10.1: *An investigator's work will be presented in the courtroom.*

The Pre-Trial Process

Once the defendant is formally charged, the court process begins. In a criminal case, the first stage is called the **first appearance**. The first appearance may or may not be in front of the court that will eventually hear the case. During this stage, a criminal defendant is advised of the charges against him and told what bail is. There is no equivalent in the civil process.

In a criminal case, **bail** (or **bond**) is the amount of money or surety (property) that a defendant must put up as collateral to be released from jail pending trial. If the defendant uses a bail bondsman to obtain bail, the bondsman usually charges between 10 and 15% to bond the individual out of jail. The fee paid to the bondsman is non-refundable. If the defendant makes his court appearances, the bond is eventually refunded. If not, it may be forfeited to the court. Some jurisdictions have a bonding schedule for various offenses. The prosecutor may ask the court to increase a bond. The basis for such a request may include the fear that the defendant may flee the jurisdiction, or that the defendant may be a risk to other people. The defendant may also ask the court to reduce the bond. In some cases, such as murder, there is no bond and in other cases, the defendant may be released without any bond. This does not apply to civil actions.

The next stage is the **preliminary** hearing which determines if probable cause exists to send the case to trial. The prosecution will call witnesses to testify about the case. Hearsay evidence is admissible during this hearing. It is not uncommon for the lead investigator to testify as to what took place during the investigation. The victim is seldom called to testify during this phase, as the investigator can testify to what the victim said or did. It is not uncommon for the defense not to call any witnesses. During this hearing, the judge must view the evidence in the light most favorable to the prosecution. If the judge determines that probable cause exists, the case will be set for trial.

The next stage in the criminal process is the **arraignment** (there is no equivalent stage in the civil process). At this stage, the defendant is formally charged with the offenses and asked to enter a plea. The pleas that the defendant may enter are:

- Not Guilty

- Guilty

- **No Contest:** defendant does not admit or deny guilt; usually part of a plea agreement

- **Not Guilty by Reason of Insanity:** the defendant is not responsible for his or her actions because of a mental illness or psychiatric state

The next stage is the **motions phase**. At this point, defense counsel presents arguments as to why certain evidence should not be admitted during the trial. The prosecution may argue for admission of various pieces of evidence, file motions for the admission of similar transactions by the defendant in earlier cases, or ask that the court require the defendant to provide non-testimonial evidence.

Once the motions hearings are over, the trial may begin. Prior to the trial, there may be one or more **status hearings**, during which the court asks counsel if there are any changes, such as additional motions or a possible plea agreement (criminal case) or settlement (civil case). In the case of a plea bargain, the prosecution and the defense come to an agreement on charges and sentencing for the defendant. In a civil settlement, the plaintiff agrees to a monetary amount from the defendant in exchange for dismissing charges.

The Trial
The first portion of the trial deals with jury selection, including *voir dire*, which is a means of determining if a potential juror has any bias that would not allow the juror to be fair to both sides. During *voir dire*, attorneys from both sides have an opportunity to question prospective jurors and determine who should sit on the jury. In

some states, the judge, rather than the attorneys, asks the majority of the questions. This is a process that may move relatively quickly or may take days.

Potential jurors may be excused from the jury in one of two ways. In order for a potential juror to be **dismissed for cause**, the court must find an articulated reason why the potential juror should be dismissed. This may include such things as knowing the defendant, knowing the investigators associated with the case, a status as a previous victim of a similar crime, or undue hardship. The other way a juror may be dismissed is by **peremptory challenges**. The prosecution and defense are given a number of challenges; the attorneys do not have to state a reason for dismissing the potential juror.

Once the jury has been empanelled, the prosecution, which has the burden of proof, has the opportunity to give an **opening statement** explaining what they intend to prove. After the prosecution concludes its opening statement, the defense has the opportunity to give an opening statement, as well. Although it is uncommon, especially in felony cases, the attorneys may waive opening statements or give them at a later time in the trial. Opening statements are not considered evidence, and are not to be used by the jury in their deliberations of the case.

After opening statements, the prosecution presents its case. Witnesses are called to testify. Testimony of a witness, including investigators, follows this format:

- The prosecutor calls the witness to the stand where the court administers an oath. In the oath, the witness swears to tell the truth.

- The prosecution begins the direct examination of the witness. During the direct examination, the prosecutor asks the witness open-ended questions. The purpose of direct examination is to provide the jury with facts relating to the case.

- After the direct examination is completed, the defense attorney begins the cross-examination. The purpose of cross-examination is to either clarify or discredit the testimony given on direct examination. Defense counsel may attempt to establish inconsistencies, biases, or other damaging facts pertaining to direct examination testimony.

- After the defense attorney completes the cross-examination, the prosecutor may re-direct. During re-direct, the prosecutor may only seek to clarify information that was presented during cross-examination. The prosecutor cannot go into new areas of testimony. After the prosecutor finishes re-direct, the defense may re-cross.

- When witnesses conclude their testimony, they are excused. The attorneys have the option of having the witness' subpoena continued, meaning that the witness may be called later in the trial. If the attorneys do not continue the witness' subpoena, the witness is excused from the trial.

This procedure repeats until the prosecution presents all its witnesses. After the prosecution finishes with its last witness, the defense may present its witnesses. The defense is not required to put on any evidence. One of the biggest decisions concerning the defense case relates to whether or not the defendant will testify. If the defendant testifies, the defense attorney calls the defendant to the stand and conducts direct examination. The defendant will then be cross-examined by the prosecution. Under certain rules of procedure, he can be asked about his criminal history, and possibly about other criminal events, depending on the circumstances.

After the defense has called all of its witnesses, the prosecution may call **rebuttal witnesses**; these individuals are called to rebut or contradict another witness' testimony.

Example

The defense puts on a witness who testifies that the victim was not afraid of the defendant, and there were never any problems between the defendant and the victim. The prosecution's rebuttal witness testifies that the victim was afraid of the defendant, and that on several occasions the defendant assaulted the victim.

After the prosecution and defense have presented their cases, the prosecutor, defense counsel, and judge compile the **jury instructions**. These are documents that set forth the elements of the crimes, the rules of evidence, and other issues that the jury must consider during their deliberation, such as burden of proof and affirmative defenses. The jury instructions are read into the court record and the jury is allowed to take the jury instructions with them during their deliberations.

Instructions can be of varying lengths. Some are standard instructions used during all trials, while other instructions may be very specific to a given case.

Once the jury instructions have been read, the attorneys will present their closing arguments. This phase is the attorneys' last opportunity to address the jury. During closing arguments, attorneys summarize the evidence and witness testimony. The prosecution also provides their view of the evidence. The prosecution will address the elements of the charged crimes and discuss how those elements were proven. The prosecution often concludes its closing argument by asking the jury to find the defendant guilty of the charges presented.

Defense counsel then presents their closing. The defense may argue that the prosecution didn't prove its case beyond a reasonable doubt. Defense counsel may ask the jury to consider various witnesses' testimony to determine if the witness is being truthful.

Most courts limit the amount of time the attorneys may use for closing. In some states the prosecution may be allowed a rebuttal closing. During the rebuttal closing, the prosecution is given the last opportunity to address the jury. In civil cases, the plaintiff's attorney is the first to present closing arguments, followed by the defense attorney.

At the conclusion of closing arguments, the jury is sent out to deliberate the case. In a criminal case, the jury determines if the prosecution proved the charged crimes beyond a reasonable doubt. If the jury determines that the prosecution did not meet that standard, the defendant is found not guilty. In civil cases, the jury is responsible for determining whether they believe the plaintiff's position or the defendant's position, and the amount, if any, of the monetary award.

The jury may find the defendant guilty of some or all of the charged offenses. A jury, if provided verdict forms for **lesser-included offenses**, may find the defendant guilty of lesser offenses and not guilty of the charged offenses.

If the criminal defendant is convicted, the next phase is **sentencing**, which refers to the punishment the defendant will receive. Sentences may be a fine, imprisonment or a combination of the two. If a defendant was found guilty of multiple charges, the sentence may be concurrent or consecutive. **Concurrent** sentences are served at the same time. **Consecutive** means that multiple sentences are served, one after the other, until all are completed.

Unique Aspects

The victim plays a critical role in the courtroom proceedings. In highly charged cases such as sexual assault, homicide, and child abuse, the victim may be very emotional. Sometimes the victim is afraid of retribution, has an emotional tie to the defendant, or is traumatized by having to recall the crime. Although the prosecutor and investigator spend a great deal of time with the victims, they may be so overwhelmed or emotional that they don't testify well. Seeing the defendant in court may enrage the victim or cause the victim to shut down.

Witnesses may also be hesitant to testify out of fear of retribution, an emotional tie to the defendant, being a co-defendant in the case or having done something that he or she is ashamed of. Like victims, witnesses may become scared or defensive during their testimony.

Concepts Associated with a Criminal Trial

In criminal cases, the defendant is presumed innocent until proven guilty. This means that the prosecution has the burden of proving that the defendant committed the crimes of which he is accused. If the prosecution is unable to meet that burden, the defendant will be found not guilty. The defendant is not required to testify, and may not even provide any evidence during the trial.

Prosecutorial discretion refers to the options the prosecution has in determining what the defendant is charged with, what will be offered to the defendant in the form of a plea agreement, and who is called to testify during the trial. A prosecutor may determine that a co-defendant will get a plea agreement in exchange for his testimony against another defendant. The ultimate discretion a prosecutor has is determining whether or not to pursue the death penalty in certain cases.

Example

Two men robbed a commercial bank in a large metropolitan area. One of the suspects drove the getaway car and the other suspect went into the bank, brandished a gun, and took the money. The prosecutor offered the driver an indeterminate sentence of two to four years, and wouldn't offer a deal to the other suspect.

The prosecutor has the burden of determining the likelihood of prevailing in a criminal case and what would be an appropriate sentence for a defendant that is willing to take a plea.

Prosecutorial misconduct is an allegation that the prosecutor abused his authority or engaged in some type of misconduct. Common allegations of prosecutorial misconduct are that the prosecution is arbitrary and/or that the prosecutor withheld evidence favorable to the defense.

Ethical codes govern how attorneys practice law. The bar association in every state regulates lawyer conduct. A defense attorney has an ethical obligation to zealously defend his client. A prosecutor has an ethical obligation to pursue only those criminal cases that he believes are reasonably likely to result in a conviction. A prosecutor also has an ethical obligation to provide defense counsel the entire discovery relating to a case.

Another concept that applies to trial is the **Rules of Evidence**, which govern the introduction of evidence in cases. In addition to addressing issues relating to the chain of evidence, the Rules of Evidence address such factors as whether the evidence is competent, material, and relevant. Evidence is considered **competent** if it is shown to be reliable, and **material** if it has a logical connection to the case. Evidence is considered to be **relevant** when it is offered to prove or disprove a fact presented during the court proceedings. Weight is how much importance the trier of the case gives to a particular piece of evidence.

Example

A defendant is charged with theft. Any potential evidence pertaining to the defendant's criminal history for assault would not be relevant to the charge of theft. The criminal history concerning assault has nothing to do with the charged crime.

Evidence of a defendant's earlier statements about being upset or getting even with the victim may be determined to be relevant, but the significance (or weight) of those earlier statements is left up to the jury. The jury may give great weight to the statements if they believe that those statements are a precursor to the defendant's alleged theft from the victim. Likewise, the jury may give little weight to the statements if they believe that people often make such statements and don't act upon them.

Types of Evidence Offered in Court

There are several general types of evidence that may be admitted during a trial. **Demonstrative evidence** illustrates the testimony of a witness and includes such things as pictures, diagrams, maps, and digital recordings. The primary purpose of such evidence is to help the jury understand the testimony of a given witness and also give

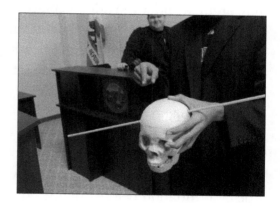

FIGURE 10.2: *Numerous types of evidence will be presented in any given trial.*

credibility to the testimony. Demonstrative evidence can be admitted into evidence through lay witnesses or expert witnesses.

Example

The lead investigator testifies as to what he found when he first arrived at the scene of the crime. The prosecutor shows the investigator various photographs of the scene and asks if the photographs accurately show what the scene looked like when the investigator was there. The photographs are then introduced into evidence.

The forensic pathologist testifies about his findings during the autopsy. The prosecutor shows the forensic pathologist pictures taken at the autopsy and an anatomical drawing that the pathologist compiled as a result of the autopsy. Once the pathologist testifies that the pictures and diagram accurately show what the pathologist found during autopsy, they are admitted into evidence.

Documentary evidence may take a variety of forms, such as contracts, letters, or diaries. The side offering the documentary evidence must show that the evidence is authentic and relevant. The opposing attorney may argue against the admissibility of such evidence, stating that the document is hearsay evidence and that the document cannot be shown to be authentic. (The concept of hearsay evidence will be addressed in a later section.) In such cases, the attorney offering the documentary evidence will have to put on testimony showing who compiled the document to show its authenticity.

Testimonial evidence is the most common type of evidence offered during a trial. Unlike documentary evidence, which often requires some type of foundation before it is introduced, testimonial evidence stands alone. The witness taking an oath swearing to tell the truth always precedes testimonial evidence.

The witness must be shown to be competent. Issues concerning competence may include the age of the witness and his or her mental condition. If a witness is testifying and needs to refresh her memory, the court may allow the witness to refer to reports containing information the witness provided to investigators. The court may also allow the attorney to ask leading questions to help refresh the witness' recall.

Testimonial evidence can either be direct or hearsay. **Hearsay evidence** is a statement or act done by someone other than the person who is testifying and is offered to prove the truth of the matter.

Example

Betty Wilcox testifies that her next-door neighbor, Eva Compton, told Ms. Wilcox that Ms. Compton saw the defendant commit the crime. This is hearsay because the Ms. Wilcox did not see the defendant commit the crime. The same would apply if Ms. Compton had heard something and told Ms. Wilcox and Ms. Wilcox testified about the statement. At trial, Ms. Wilcox would not be allowed to testify about Ms. Compton's observations or statements.

There are many exceptions to the hearsay rule. A few of those exceptions warrant discussion here. **Excited utterances** are statements made by a person in response to a traumatic event. **Dying declarations** are statements made by a person who is aware that he/she is dying. Out-of-court identification statements concerning the identification of a person will be admitted.

Example

Excited Utterance: A police officer arrives on the scene of a reported homicide. A woman runs out of the house and screams, "He killed them all!" The officer will be allowed to testify to the woman's statement.

Dying Declaration: A man is stabbed in his apartment and stumbles to the next-door neighbor's house. The neighbor calls the police who arrive and attempt to render aid to the stabbed man. The stabbed man tells officers that he knows he is dying and says, "Jackie stabbed me." The victim then dies. The officer could testify as to what the victim told the officer.

Out of Court Identification Statement: The lead detective showed the victim a photographic lineup that contained a picture of the defendant. The victim picked out the picture of the defendant as being the person who assaulted her and said, "That's him. I am sure of it." The detective could testify as to what the victim said during the lineup.

Defenses in Criminal Cases

In a criminal case, the defendant has two basic defenses: either he didn't commit the crime in question, or he did it, but there is some reason for him committing the crime. The defendant's reason for committing the crime is presented in the form of an affirmative defense. In an **affirmative defense**, the defendant admits that the crime occurred, but offers a defense that either mitigates or justifies the defendant's action. Affirmative defenses are presented by defense counsel to the court and must be done in a timely manner, meaning that the notice of an affirmative defense must be stated early enough in the proceedings that the prosecution can prepare to dispute it. If the defense attorney does not file notice of the affirmative defense in a timely manner, the alternative defense option is considered to be waived. The most common affirmative defense is self-defense. By asserting self-defense, the defendant is contending that he had a reasonable belief that unlawful force was being used against him, and that he had to respond with force to either protect himself or others. A defendant who asserts an affirmative defense may or may not testify at trial; his attorney will present his defense and explanation.

Example

Peter Jones is charged with first degree murder in the death of a neighbor, John Smith. Jones asserts the affirmative defense of self-defense. He contends that Smith initiated a confrontation with Jones and that during the confrontation, Smith pulled a knife and attempted to stab Jones. Jones contends that he took the knife away from Smith; during the struggle, Jones stabbed Smith.

Other types of affirmative defenses are: insanity, intoxication, duress, entrapment, battered woman syndrome or necessity. The use of affirmative defenses may vary from state to state. Although affirmative defenses are raised by the defense, prosecutors must still disprove the case.

Investigators need to be aware of these possible defenses and address them during the course of the investigation. It is just as important to exonerate an innocent person as it is to convict someone who committed a wrongful act. While the following is not an all-inclusive list, it provides a sampling of how to address some of the affirmative and alibi defenses:

Alibis

Another defense strategy is the **alibi**; here, the defense contends the defendant could not have committed the crime because she was not present when the crime occurred. Defense counsel must provide notice to the prosecution of the intent to present alibi information, thus allowing the prosecution the opportunity to negate the alibi defense.

Investigators should interview all potential alibi witnesses and attempt to find corroborating information supporting the alibi defense. For instance: if the defendant contends that he was with his girlfriend at a motel, the investigator should obtain a detailed statement from the girlfriend, contact other individuals who could verify that the defendant and the witness were together, obtain receipts from the motel, and identify any reasons why the witness may attempt to lie for the defendant.

Example

Example A - Battered Woman Syndrome:
If there is evidence that the defendant abused the victim, the investigator must provide that information to the defense. The investigator should also obtain specific information concerning earlier incidents and what the defendant did in response to those incidents.

A major consideration in cases of battered woman syndrome is the concept of imminent danger, which means that the person is in danger at the time of the incident. If the prosecution establishes that the defendant committed the alleged crimes based upon the victim's previous acts or in anticipation of future abuse by the victim, the jury may find that the affirmative defense does not apply.

Example

Example B - Voluntary Intoxication:

States vary on the use of voluntary intoxication as a defense. In some states, voluntary intoxication does not apply as an affirmative defense to first degree murder. During the course of the investigation, the investigator should try to determine if the defendant was drinking and, if so, the level of intoxication. In cases other than traffic offenses, investigators may have to obtain a warrant to draw the defendant's blood to determine his blood alcohol level.

Subpoenas

A **subpoena** is a writ compelling a person to testify in a court proceeding. Either party may issue subpoenas. Either law enforcement or a process server may serve the potential witness. If the person who was subpoenaed fails to show up in court on the designated court date, the court may issue a bench warrant for failure to appear.

Previously discussed in Module Four, a *subpoena duces tecum* is a subpoena that compels a person to produce documents to the court regarding a specific case. Often the **custodian of records**, meaning the person who has control of the documents on behalf of an agency or organization, responds to the court.

Depending on the state, there are various restrictions concerning when, how and to whom subpoenas must be served. Most courts require a reasonable amount of time between the time that the subpoena was served and the court hearing. It would be unreasonable to serve a witness on Sunday night for a Monday morning hearing. If the court determines that the service was unreasonable, the witness does not have to appear.

When a person is served with a subpoena, the server must fill out a return showing when, where and to whom the subpoena was served. Some jurisdictions require that the server sign the return and that the server's signature is notarized.

Preparing for Trial

From an investigator's perspective, preparation for trial is broken into two areas: preparing the case for trial and preparing herself for trial. In preparing the case for trial, the investigator will meet with the prosecutor handling the case many times in order to go over the various aspects of the case. Some of the areas that the investigator and prosecutor will address are:

- Has all of the forensic evidence been tested?

- Has all of the evidence been inventoried?

- Have subpoenas been served on all of the State's witnesses?

- Have the potential defense witnesses been interviewed?

- Are there any leads that have not been pursued?

- Does the prosecution need any demonstrative evidence?

- Who would be the best witness to introduce various pieces of evidence?

The prosecutor, sometimes accompanied by an investigator, will meet with the State's witnesses and review their testimony. If new information is obtained during these meetings, or as a result of an investigator doing some additional work, the newly discovered information must be turned over to the defense.

Testifying

Testifying is the culmination of the investigative process; it can also be one of the most challenging aspects of an investigation. During the investigation, the investigator is in control of the situation. While there may be a supervisor asking why certain actions were taken, there is not the same type of scrutiny that a defense attorney may engage in at trial. Just the formality of a courtroom setting can be unnerving to an investigator.

FIGURE 10.3: *Testifying at trial is an essential part of an investigator's duties.*

As with any new situation, an investigator may be uncomfortable the first time he testifies. Seasoned investigators should not get too comfortable, as they may think that they don't have to prepare.

The most important thing for an investigator to remember concerning testifying is to always tell the truth. Investigators should also:

Be prepared. Remembering what the investigator did during the course of the investigation is critical. An investigator will not be allowed to read from notes, although the investigator may refresh his recollection by looking briefly at a report. Jurors and the prosecutor expect investigators to be able to testify from memory and refer to reports on a very limited basis. As part of the preparation, the investigator should meet with the prosecutor and go over the questions, or at least the areas, that the prosecutor will ask about. Knowing what the prosecutor will ask will help the investigator be more comfortable on the stand.

Dress and act professionally. All investigators should wear conservative, business-style clothing. The jury looks at an investigator as the representative of the victims. If the investigator doesn't dress professionally, or act in a professional manner, the defense attorney may make inferences that the investigation itself may be unprofessional. Other examples of acting professional are:

- Answering confidently

- Using "yes" or "no" rather than "yeah" or "nah"

- Behaving attentively during the proceedings

Helpful hints for time spent on the witness stand include:

DO	DO NOT
Act confident	Behave in an arrogant or argumentative fashion
Maintain a serious demeanor	Get defensive or angry during questioning
Speak clearly	Chew gum
Maintain eye contact	Try to anticipate the line of questioning
Listen to the full question posed before responding	Give opinions (unless acting as an expert witness)
Remember there is no such thing as "off the record" with an attorney or reporter	Use police jargon or legalese
Correct errors or misstatements made on the stand immediately	Guess or estimate; if the answer is unknown, say so

Discovery

Discovery pertains to the process of providing case information to the defense. Discovery starts once the case has been filed and the defendant has counsel. It is the responsibility of the prosecution to provide the defense with all investigative reports, statements, videotapes, scientific analysis, and evidence information. Failure to comply with discovery may lead to sanctions against the prosecution, which could include exclusion of evidence at trial.

Complying with discovery is also the responsibility of the criminal investigators. If prosecutors don't know about certain information, it is impossible for them to comply with the requirement of discovery. Investigators should have a system by which every potential item that may be subject to discovery is made known to the prosecution. In many jurisdictions, the investigator is required to provide the prosecutor with all known discovery at the time criminal charges are filed. This should include copies of any discs or tapes. The problem may arise subsequent to the filing, when the investigator conducts follow-up investigations and obtains additional information. Once the case is filed, the investigator should have periodic meetings with the prosecutor to ensure that all new information is provided to the defense.

Attorney work product is not discoverable. **Work product** is the attorney's impressions, research, or theories concerning the case, not the actual product of the investigation.

Exculpatory Information

Exculpatory information is information that may absolve or exonerate the defendant. Any exculpatory information that is developed during the course of the investigation must be provided to the prosecution, who must in turn provide it to the defense. There is no requirement that the defendant ask for any exculpatory information. If it is later learned that exculpatory information existed and the prosecution did not provide such information to the defendant, the case may be reversed. There may also be sanctions against the prosecutor and/or the investigator who had knowledge about the exculpatory evidence and did not provide it to the defense.

Example

The prosecution had information that the defendant was incarcerated in a different county at the time the alleged crime occurred. The investigator confirmed that the defendant was incarcerated at the time of the offense, but did not provide that information to the prosecutor.

When defense counsel later learned that the investigator knew about the incarceration and didn't provide the information to defense counsel, sanctions were brought against the investigator.

Sometimes an investigator may be hesitant to provide potential exculpatory information because the investigator doesn't consider the information to be exculpatory. If there is any doubt, the investigator should err on the side of caution and provide the information to the prosecutor and thus to the defense.

Privileged Information

Privileged information is confidential information. The basic premise concerning privileged information is that certain types of communication cannot be divulged without consent of the parties, though there are some legal exceptions to the policy. Some of the more common types of privileged communication are:

- Attorney-Client

- Doctor-Patient

- Clergy-Parishioner

- Husband-Wife

- Psychologist-Client

The communication aspect in such situations goes only to verbal communication, not to physical actions.

Example

A patient comes into a hospital with multiple gunshot wounds. The physician can tell investigators the nature of the wounds and that the patient needs surgery. Any communication between the doctor and patient in the course of the patient's treatment would be privileged.

CASE STUDY

The police responded to a domestic violence call at 237 Grant Street. When the police arrived, they found John Williams lying on the ground outside that address. Mr. Williams told the responding officers that his girlfriend, Yvonne Clark, had stabbed him. Mr. Williams told the officers that he had stabbed Yvonne and that she was still inside the residence.

When the officers went inside the residence, they found Yvonne Clark on the floor of the master bedroom. She had seven stab wounds to her chest and arms. Paramedics arrived and pronounced Ms. Clark dead.

One of the people contacted by the police was Mr. Williams' sister, who stated she had received a telephone call from Mr. Williams in which he stated he had "done it this time." He also told his sister that he had "lost it" and stabbed Ms. Clark.

Mr. Williams was charged with second degree murder. His defense was "self-defense" and "provocation," alleging that Ms. Clark had started the argument that led to her death.

- What are the potential problems with this case?

- What evidence would you need if you were on the prosecution team?

- What evidence would you need if you were on the defense team?

- What would you tell the jury if you were on the prosecution team? The defense team?

FIGURE 10.4: *Whether an investigator is working for the prosecution/plaintiff or the defense, it is exciting to see the investigation finally bear fruit.*

Summary

The trial is the culmination of all the work that went into an investigation. Mistakes made in preparation of, or during, the trial can have a monumental effect on the outcome. If the investigation is done well, the chances of prevailing in trial are greatly enhanced.

In criminal cases, the standard that must be met to convict the defendant is beyond a reasonable doubt. In civil cases, the standard that must be met to prevail is preponderance. In criminal cases, the prosecution has the burden of meeting the standard, while in civil cases, the plaintiff has the burden of meeting the standard.

In criminal cases, the prosecution presents its case first, after which the defense puts on its case. Either side may call lay and expert witnesses, and each side has the opportunity to cross-examine witnesses that testify. The defendant has the choice of testifying or not testifying. The jury cannot consider whether or not the defendant testifies as part of their deliberations.

The jury can find the defendant guilty or not guilty. If the jury cannot reach a unanimous decision, the prosecution has to decide to either re-try the defendant or dismiss the charges.

Testifying is the final stage of the investigator's role in a case. How the investigator handles himself during his testimony is critical. Although there are a number of things that an investigator can do to make his testimony more effective, the two most important things are to be prepared and to testify truthfully.

Exculpatory evidence and discovery violations are two major factors that can cause major problems during a trial. Any information obtained during the course of the trial that may exonerate the defendant must be made available to defense counsel as soon as possible.

Discussion Questions

1. Discuss the importance of the role of the following individuals in a criminal case:

   a. Victim
   b. Investigator
   c. Prosecutor
   d. Defense Attorney

2. Everything that the prosecution obtains during the course of the investigation must be provided to the defense. Should the defense be required to provide the prosecution with everything the defense obtains?

3. Are there some types of privileged information that should be admitted during trial? What types should be admitted? Why?

4. Evidence is admitted and excluded from a trial. Discuss whether or not juries get "the whole picture" to make a just decision. Discuss the advantages and disadvantages of allowing all evidence in.

5. Discuss the benefits and disadvantages of plea-bargaining. Should certain types of crimes not qualify for plea-agreement? Is justice better served through plea-agreements or trials?

Exercises

1. Write a paper addressing the pros and cons of plea agreements. Should repeat offenders be allowed to plea bargain? Are there some crimes that should not allow plea bargaining as an option?

2. Research a civil case where punitive damages in excess of $1 million were awarded. Does this seem excessive? Why or why not?

3. Go to a local district court house and watch a criminal trial for an hour. Describe the roles of the various "players" in the trial. How does a real trial compare to a television portrayal?

4. Research what types of affirmative defenses are available to a defendant. List and give an explanation of three affirmative defenses. Write a two page paper addressing if defendants should be allowed to use affirmative defenses.

5. Research the various types of hearsay that is admissible in court. Give three examples. State your position as to whether or not hearsay should always be admissible.

Key Terms

Actual Damages: monetary amount intended to compensate a plaintiff for expenses.

Adversarial System: a court system where two opposing parties argue a case in front of an impartial party, either a judge or jury.

Affirmative Defense: a trial strategy wherein the defendant admits to committing a crime but offers a reason that either mitigates or justifies the defendant's action.

Arraignment: the stage of the court process where the defendant is formally charged with an offense.

Bail: the amount of money or surety the defendant must put up to be released from jail.

Closing Argument: a summary of the evidence each party presents to the jury at the conclusion of all of the evidence.

Competent Evidence: evidence that is deemed reliable.

Concurrent Sentence: a sentence where two or more sentences are served at the same time.

Consecutive Sentences: multiple sentences are served one after the other until all are completed.

Cross-Examination: the questioning of a witness after the witness has concluded direct testimony.

Custodian of Records: the individual who maintains control over specific records on behalf of an agency or organization.

Demonstrative Evidence: used to help explain the testimony of a witness.

- Examples include: photographs and three-dimensional models.

Discovery: the requirement that all documentation/evidence obtained during the course of an investigation is provided to the defense.

Direct Examination: the initial questioning of a witness during trial.

Documentary Evidence: paper evidence that is offered to support or negate a premise.

Dying Declaration: a hearsay exception in which a dying person's statement as to who caused the death is admitted into court.

Excited Utterance: statement made by a person in response to a traumatic event.

Hearsay Evidence: a statement or act done by someone other than the person testifying.

Hung Jury: when the jury is unable to reach a unanimous verdict.

Jury Instructions: instructions the court gives to the jury before the jury begins their deliberation.

Lesser Included Offense: a criminal act that has some, but not all of the elements of a higher charge. For example, Second Degree Murder is a lesser-included offense of First Degree Murder.

Material Evidence: evidence that has a logical connection to a case.

No Contest: defendant does not admit or deny guilt; usually part of a plea agreement.

Not Guilty By Reason of Insanity: the defendant is not responsible for his or her actions because of a mental illness or psychiatric state.

Opening Statements: the opportunity for each party to tell the jury what it believes the evidence will show.

Peremptory Challenges: when an attorney excuses a potential juror without having to state a reason for the dismissal.

Plaintiff: the party who brings a suit in civil court.

Prosecutorial Discretion: the discretion granted to prosecutors in determining who is charged, what the charges will be, and possible plea agreements.

Prosecutorial Misconduct: allegation that the prosecution abused its authority or engaged in some misconduct.

Punitive Damages: awarded as punishment in a civil case.

Rebuttal Closing: the last opportunity the prosecution has to address the jury, after the defense's closing arguments. Only relevant in certain states.

Rebuttal Witness: a witness called to testify for the purpose of rebutting or contradicting what another witness testified to.

Relevancy: evidence offered to prove or disprove a fact presented during a court proceeding.

Rules of Evidence: the rules governing the admissibility of evidence in a court proceeding.

Status Hearing: a stage of the court proceedings where both sides advise the judge of the status of the case; for instance, whether a potential resolution has been reached or the parties will proceed to trial.

Subpoena: a writ compelling a person to testify in court.

Trier of the Facts: the judge or jury that determines guilt or innocence in a criminal case and damages in a civil case.

Tort: a civil wrong.

Voir Dire: the questioning of potential jurors by attorneys to determine who should serve.

Work Product: an attorney's impressions, research, or theories regarding a case; work product is not discoverable.

Notes